Creed for a Young Catholic

CREED for a YOUNG CATHOLIC

RICHARD CHILSON

NAZARETH BOOKS
Doubleday & Company, Inc.
Garden City, New York
1981

ISBN: 0-385-17436-5
Library of Congress Catalog Card Number: 80-2073
Copyright © 1981 by The Catholic Heritage Press, Inc.
All Rights Reserved
Printed in the United States of America
First Edition

For Gregory
   across ten thousand years

Other titles in series:

Keeping a Spiritual Journal
Am I OK—If I Feel the Way I Do?
That We Might Have Life
With Their Whole Strength
A Young Person's Book of Catholic Words

Contents

1. We Believe — 9
2. We Believe in One God — 21
3. We Believe in Jesus Christ — 43
4. We Believe in the Holy Spirit — 85
5. Bringing the Creed into Our Hearts — 115

1.

We Believe

When Jesus was a boy of twelve, his mother and father took him to Jerusalem for the great feast of Passover. For Jesus' people, Jerusalem was the real center of the world. King David had built the city many centuries before, and David's son, King Solomon, had constructed and dedicated the magnificent temple there. The Jewish people considered it a great privilege and honor to be able to celebrate the Passover in Jerusalem. To this day, each year they make a wish that they might be able to spend the following Passover in Jerusalem. "Next year in Jerusalem," they say to one another.

Jesus set out with Mary and Joseph on the three-day journey to the holy city. They walked and camped with relatives and friends or even strangers who were also making the pilgrimage. By day they walked, and by night they camped near the road. Around the fires, Jesus listened to the stories about the holy city and the great temple. The closer the group came to their destination, the more excited Jesus grew. Surely this would be the greatest Passover of his life!

Once they arrived in Jerusalem, Jesus and his parents went directly to the temple. Here God's presence dwelt among his people. This was God's house, the holiest place on earth. Throughout the temple courtyards Jesus saw the doctors and teachers of the Law arguing with one another. These were the most learned men of Israel, for their knowledge was of God.

All along the journey Jesus had been most anxious to go to the temple, for he wanted to hear these wise men speak of God. During the week of the Passover feast the families went each day to the temple. Jesus listened to the doctors and priests speaking of the complex questions of the Law. Each day, sitting in the temple courtyards, Jesus listened to the arguments flowing back and forth from learned head to learned head. He absorbed their knowledge and wisdom, but he said nothing. He was a boy of twelve. What could he possibly say to these great teachers of God's Law?

When the Passover ended and the pilgrims prepared to leave Jerusalem and return home, Jesus was so caught up in the life and activities of the temple that he forgot the feast was over. By then he knew how to make his way to the temple on his own. He didn't have to depend on his parents to take him. He would walk to the temple early in the morning and spend the entire day there absorbed in the talk and debate.

One particular day was to be different. On this day Jesus no longer simply listened. He dared to speak to these great teachers, the wisest men in Israel, about God. What could this twelve-year-old boy say that would make these teachers take heed and listen to him? They already knew the Law. They had studied and pondered and argued it more than any men alive in Israel. Their whole lives had been devoted to the study and knowledge of God. Nothing was considered of more importance.

Perhaps Jesus didn't speak to them of anything

they did not already know. Maybe he reminded them of things that in their complex arguments they had forgotten. Jesus spoke to these doctors and teachers of the Law from the knowledge of his heart, not from the knowledge of his head. They too had known such wisdom when they, like Jesus, were young. But as adults, more demanding and difficult questions occupied their time so that they lost sight of the simple truths that children know.

Jesus spoke as the prophets before him, not out of great learning, but out of simple understanding. He spoke of things learned at home in Nazareth. He told of the love of God that Mary and Joseph had shared with him. He spoke of God's mercy and constant love that he had learned in school as his teachers unfolded the Scriptures and told again the marvelous story of God's unshakable love for Israel. There was no talk here of complex questions of the Law: how far a person could journey on the Sabbath; what were the different kinds of sacrifices; or when the Messiah would come. These were important issues, but not as important as the pure love of God that Jesus revealed with his straightforward twelve-year-old words.

We, like those teachers of the Law, are familiar with the things Jesus said. We have learned of God's love as Jesus did from our family and our church.

As we grow older and leave childhood behind, we are often tempted to forget the simple truths we know so well. In the difficult world of growing up, we may even wonder whether these things are really true. We will meet many people who will claim they are not true. Others will believe but not as we do. So as we take on all the complex ways of adults, we, like those doctors of the Law, may come to feel that life is more mysterious and complicated than we thought it was when we were children. In our hard-won knowledge of deep things, we may forget the teachings of the heart that can show us happiness and enable us to live a full life.

Yet we need not forget the wonderful wisdom of which Jesus spoke. We can carry it with us in the words of the Creed. Christians have reduced to a few words all the wisdom that is important for us to remember. These words and the beautiful stories we have heard about Jesus and God can lead us to happiness. Holding these truths in our hearts, we will never feel lost, for we know how near we are to the God who loves us, cares for us, and wishes to bring us home.

What did Jesus say to these elders of Israel? What did he tell these men so knowledgeable in the Law? He may have reminded them that it is not so important to have knowledge about God as it is to have faith and trust in him. Jesus had heard many stories about God and Israel in his school. One story must have made a deep impression on him, for it concerned a man whose trust in God was so great that everyone in Israel looked to him as their ancestor and father: they called him Father Abraham.

However, when we first meet Abraham in the

story, he is not yet a father. At the beginning he was living in the city of Ur and his name was Abram. He and his wife Sarah were good citizens. They probably owned a house and were rather well-off. Then one day something disturbed the calm of Abram and Sarah's life. Abram heard a voice.

"Take Sarah, your wife, and leave this city," the voice demanded. "I will lead you to a new land; there I will make you the father of a great nation."

Imagine yourself in Abram's situation. He was comfortable where he was. He had a good job, a nice house, a loving wife. Why should he abandon all this to obey a voice that came out of nowhere? Was the voice really from God? Perhaps it was a trick. Maybe Abram was hearing things. How could he know whether the things the voice promised would indeed come true?

But Abram trusted the voice. He really trusted in God. So he and Sarah sold their house, packed a few belongings, and set off into the desert. For many years they journeyed through deserts and across mountains. They had no idea where they were headed, only that the voice had told them to keep going. Finally the voice told Abram that they had reached the spot where he and Sarah should build their new home. Here was the land that was promised them.

Weary from the hardships of travel, Abram and Sarah were grateful that their trek was over. They settled on the land and made a new life for themselves. Then the voice told Abram that he would become a father and that his descendants would be as numerous as the stars of the sky or the sands of the seashore. Abram had been chosen by God to be a father of his great people. In honor of his new fatherhood, Abram received a new name. From then on he was known as Abraham. Our names carry much of who we are. When our life takes a different direction such as moving to a new country or speaking a different language, we may change our name as well.

Abraham was delighted with the promise that he would become a father, but it didn't seem possible, for he was already very old and Sarah was far beyond the age when she could bear children.

How can I possibly become the father of many peoples? Abraham often wondered to himself as time went by. Indeed, years passed, and nothing happened. Finally Abraham decided that if God intended him to have children he'd better do something to help, so he adopted a child. This will be the child of the promise, thought Abraham.

Then, once again, after all those years, Abraham heard the voice. The voice repeated the promise that Abraham would be the father of many nations, and furthermore that the child of the promise would be Abraham and Sarah's child.

Sarah happened to be outside the tent as the voice addressed Abraham. She could not help overhearing, and she began to laugh at such a ridiculous idea. "Why are you laughing, Sarah?" asked the voice. Sarah quickly regained her seriousness and said that she had not been laughing at all.

Abraham and Sarah both knew that what the voice had promised was impossible. Now their faith was put to the test. Could they believe they would have a child? And when? Neither of them was growing any younger. Yet, in spite of everything, they clung to the hope that the promises would be fulfilled.

And the promises were fulfilled. Abraham and Sarah had a son, and they called him Isaac, meaning "one who laughs." Now, after their long journey, after all the waiting and uncertainty, God's promises had come to pass.

No son was loved more than Isaac. He was a wonderful child. Sarah's heart leaped with joy whenever she was near him, and Abraham felt young again in spite of his years. Isaac was truly God's gift to Sarah and Abraham, the reward for their trust and obedience.

One day the voice spoke to Abraham: "Take your young son, Isaac, and tomorrow set out for the high places where you usually make sacrifices to God. When you come to the altar, place Isaac upon it. Sacrifice him to God in thanksgiving for all God has given to you and Sarah."

Abraham was crushed. How could he kill this son whom he loved more than anything in the world? And what about God's promise that his descendants would be as numerous as the stars? Had God forgotten the promise? How could it be fulfilled if Abraham had to kill his only son? Was the voice a trick? Was it misleading him? How could he trust this voice and commit this horrid deed?

Once more, just as he had done many years ago, Abraham trusted in God. He did not know where God was leading him, but he had faith, and he decided to obey the voice. He couldn't bear to tell Sarah what he had to do, so early the next morning Abraham took Isaac and set out for the high places.

As they walked in the early-morning light, Isaac sang and played along the path. The boy's joy and vitality broke his father's heart. How can I kill my only son? he thought. What of God's promise?

At last they climbed to the high places. "But, father, where is the animal for our sacrifice?" asked Isaac. "We have forgotten to bring one with us."

Abraham couldn't speak. He took Isaac in his arms and kissed him. Then he tied the boy's hands together and placed him on the altar. Everything Abraham ever dreamed of was about to be destroyed. God had promised to make him the father of many peoples, yet now had demanded that this son of the promise die.

As Abraham raised his knife, he heard the voice once again. "Abraham, your faith has saved you. Do not slay Isaac whom you love. See, there is a ram caught in the bushes. Sacrifice the animal instead. You trusted in God even when you could not see where it would lead. God rewards your trust. He will never take Isaac from you, and Isaac will have children to delight your heart. Thousands of years from now, Abraham, millions of people will call you their father in faith because you trusted in God even when you were most helpless and confused."

Abraham freed his son, and together they sacrificed the ram in thanksgiving. On the way home, their hearts were aflame with joy, for they knew that God would help them, stand by them, and be faithful to his promises. Abraham gave thanks for the voice that so many years ago had called him to this new land, for Sarah who had come with him on the hard journey, and for Isaac who had been promised and was now given to him again as a sign of God's love and favor.

Perhaps that day in the temple, Jesus spoke to the teachers of the Law about Abraham's faith. Jesus may have reminded these great men that it is not so important to know about God as it is trust in his goodness. And as they listened to Jesus, who was probably not much older than Isaac had been on that fatal day of the sacrifice, the doctors of the Law once more felt God's love for them.

Jesus had told the wise men nothing they did not already know. They had known all their lives the importance of loving God. Each morning they said the Shema in which they confessed that they should love God with all their heart, all their soul, and all their might. But somehow, in the midst of the big concerns of the temple and its laws, they had lost sight of that love. The words of our Creed can keep us mindful of the truly important things in the midst of all the busy noise of day-to-day living.

I believe in God, the Father Almighty,
    Creator of heaven and Earth.
And in Jesus Christ,
    his only Son, our Lord;
    who was conceived of the
    Holy Spirit,
    born of the Virgin Mary,
    he suffered under Pontius Pilate,
    was crucified,
    dead and was buried.

    He descended into hell;
    the third day he rose again
    from the dead;
    He ascended into Heaven
    and sits at the right hand
    of the Father,
    from there he shall come
    to judge the living and
    the dead.

I believe in the Holy Spirit,
    the holy Catholic Church,
    the forgiveness of sins,
    the resurrection of the body
    and life everlasting.

2.
We Believe in One God

who brings meaning into our life

Abraham put his trust in God and became the father in faith for many nations. But who was this God in whom Abraham trusted? Many centuries later, another man named Moses would meet this same God and come to know him. Moses became a great leader of the children of Abraham.

The descendants of Abraham had grown to number thousands, and they had become enslaved to the people of Egypt. The Egyptians were harsh and cruel masters who forced Abraham's people to make bricks from mud and work at other heavy chores.

Moses had been raised as an Egyptian, but somehow he knew in his heart that he really belonged to this enslaved people of Israel. One day when Moses was out walking he saw an Egyptian mistreating a slave. Moses stepped in and tried to make peace, but the Egyptian grew violent, and Moses struck him. The Egyptian died instantly.

Afraid the Egyptians would discover that he was really a Jew, a slave, Moses fled from Egypt into the country of Midian where he stayed with a shepherd and helped tend the sheep. He fell in love with the shepherd's daughter and married her, but Moses could not settle down in that life. He was unhappy, for he couldn't forget that his people were condemned to harsh lives under the whips of the Egyptians. Still, he was far from

Egypt now, and there was nothing he could do to help. He could never return because he was guilty of murder. He had to sit by helplessly while his people suffered.

One day as he was tending his sheep, Moses noticed a strange sight high up on a mountain. Climbing up the slope to investigate, he came upon a bush that was burning yet was not being consumed. Here was a wonder indeed!

From the bush a voice spoke to Moses, "I am the God of your father; the God of Abraham, Isaac, and Jacob. I have heard the cries of my people suffering in Egypt. I will send you back into Egypt so that you can lead my people to freedom."

Like Abraham, Moses had met God. And as with Abraham, God demanded faith from Moses. Moses had to trust that God could lead the slaves to freedom. As God broke into Moses' life new meaning colored Moses' quiet existence. No longer would Moses have to sit and worry about his people in Egypt, for now he was called by God to rescue them.

When God entered Moses' and Abraham's lives, their lives took on new meaning and purpose. The same thing happens when God enters our lives. God brings us a vision of a better, fuller, and happier life than we had before. Now our life has purpose and direction. We know where we are headed; we know what is important for us. We learn from God what our life is all about.

And when we have faith in God, we entrust our lives to him: he becomes our guide, our leader.

We might think that once God enters our life things become simple and easy, but such is seldom the case. God's guidance is often puzzling and disturbing. Once Moses met God in the burning bush, he could not simply return to his sheep and live as before. He had to set off for Egypt and try to accomplish the impossible. It was up to one man, Moses, who had no apparent power to free his people from the grip of the most powerful person in the world, the Pharaoh of Egypt. Moses didn't seem to have the slightest chance of success. No one would bet on his side. The only possible way he could free the slaves was with the help of God. But how would God help him? Moses did not know. Like Abraham, he had to live by faith.

who brings us into freedom

Moses returned to his tents and prepared for his journey. He said good-bye to his wife and father-in-law and promised that he would come back for them once his task was done. Then he set off across the sandy waste for the land of Egypt and the struggle for freedom.

In Egypt, using all the strength and courage God had given him, Moses boldly entered the palace and went right up to Pharaoh himself.

"The God of my people has seen their misery and suffering. He demands that you let us leave Egypt so that we might worship our God, and he will provide us with a new land and a new home."

You can imagine that Pharaoh was not exactly enthusiastic about such an idea. He couldn't let a bunch of slaves free just because they demanded it. Who would be left to do the dirty work? Pharaoh found the whole idea ridiculous, and he told Moses so.

Moses was prepared for such an answer. He knew he would have to use God's power to convince Pharaoh to free the slaves. Moses threw his staff down before Pharaoh, and it turned into a frightening snake. The people in the court were terrified.

"But that's very easy to do," said Pharaoh's own magicians and they repeated the trick themselves.

Then Moses stretched forth his arm and all the waters of the Nile River turned into blood. Pharaoh was impressed, but not yet convinced.

Each day Moses returned and repeated his command to let the people go. Each day Pharaoh refused, and Moses called down another plague upon Egypt to soften Pharaoh's heart.

There was a plague of frogs—in the streets and in the bedrooms. To no avail. Moses brought in gnats, little insects that flew into everyone's face, bit them, and made them itch. Still to no avail. After that there was a plague of flies which was even more annoying than the gnats. Still Pharaoh did not give in. God sent a plague that killed the cattle, but Pharaoh remained stubborn. God afflicted everyone with boils, huge painful sores; then great hailstones damaged the crops and the houses. When Pharaoh still remained firm, God sent a cloud of locusts—insects that devoured the plants and trees. Finally, darkness descended over all the land of Egypt and everyone was frightened.

But Pharaoh would not change his mind. He would not let the slaves go free.

Moses warned Pharaoh that God would bring one final plague upon Egypt. Every firstborn child in the land of Egypt would die. What a horrible thought! Still, Pharaoh refused to listen. "I will not let the people go," he told Moses.

"Very well then; you have brought this misfortune upon yourself," replied Moses.

Moses instructed his people to kill a young lamb and smear the blood on each of their doorposts that night. "God will pass over Egypt tonight, and he will slay the firstborn children wherever they are. But we are his people, and he will see the blood on our doorposts. He will pass over our houses and spare us any suffering."

The people did as Moses directed, and during the night, the power of God passed over the entire land of Egypt. Wherever it passed, the firstborn children died. Egypt was awake with the screams of parents mourning the death of their beloved children. Only in the houses of the slaves was there no sound of mourning, for God had passed over their houses and spared them the plague.

Pharaoh was shaken and broken. The plague had not even spared his own house, and his young son lay dead in his mother's arms.

Pharaoh summoned Moses. "You and your God have won. Take your people and leave Egypt. I will let them go."

Moses gathered all his people together. "We are leaving Egypt today," he told them. "God will lead us out of slavery and into a new land that he has promised us. Gather up only the belongings you can carry with you, for we must leave before Pharaoh has a chance to change his mind."

Sure enough, Pharaoh did change his mind. He called all his armies and his chariots, and off they went in pursuit of the fleeing slaves.

Early in their flight, Moses and his people found themselves stopped by a great body of water. They had come to the sea. Pharaoh and his chariots were coming fast upon them, but they had no way of crossing this great sea.

Moses stretched out his staff over the sea and prayed. Soon a great wind arose and the waters were blown apart. In the middle of the sea there appeared a path for the people to walk across. Once more, God rescued his people and showed his determination to bring them into freedom. The people passed through the sea to the other side.

Pharaoh's chariots and his soldiers were close behind. They plunged into the path in the sea after the people, but the chariots' wheels became stuck. Here was one time it was better to be on foot than on wheels. The Egyptians were stuck hopelessly in the mud, and when the wind died, the water returned to its place and Pharaoh's entire army was drowned.

From the other side, as Moses and the people watched the destruction of the Egyptians, they gave thanks to God for rescuing them from the slavery of Egypt and for leading them into the joyous life of freedom.

Our God leads us to freedom. He is always on the side of the poor and enslaved. He loves all his people, but his heart goes out to those who are suffering and cannot enjoy the freedom he wants to give them. Our God is on the side of all those who are not free. He leads them to freedom just as he did those slaves so many thousands of years ago.

A few years ago in this country God sent another man who, like Moses, led his people out of the slavery of discrimination and hatred into the freedom of other Americans. Martin Luther King saw that black people did not have the same freedom as other Americans. They were not able to go to the same schools as others. They could not be hired for the same jobs as white people, and often they could not even eat at the same restaurants or go to the same movies.

Once again God sided with his suffering people. And through the faith and courage of Martin Luther King, the black people began their final march toward the freedom and equality God desires for all his people. As on the journey out of slavery in Egypt so long ago, there have been many trials along the way; even today the journey toward freedom of our black brothers and sisters is not over. Martin Luther King lost his life in the struggle, but he will be remembered because, like Moses, he believed and trusted in the God who leads us to freedom, who loves us, and who wants to share with us all he has to give.

who shows us how to live together in peace

Once the people had escaped the Egyptians, Moses led them to the foot of a high mountain called Sinai where he climbed up the mountain alone. On the mountain, God revealed to Moses the Law by which the people should live. The Law was created to help the people, for God intended that his people should enjoy the freedom and happiness he had given them. If they lived according to the Law, they would form a nation in which each person might live in freedom and grow in the love and knowledge of God.

On Mount Sinai, Moses—and through him the people—learned about God's plans for their future. God wants us to be happy and grow in our freedom. He loves not only each one of us, but he loves us as a nation, a people. He gives us the Law to help us live our lives. By following this Law, we and our friends and neighbors can live together in peace.

The heart of the Law is the Ten Commandments. Some of these commandments might be hard for us to understand right now. But it is enough if we remember that they are all meant to help us live a good and happy life. Following is the list of the commandments:

1. I am the Lord your God; you shall have no other gods before me.
2. You shall not take the name of the Lord your God in vain.
3. Remember the Lord's day and keep it holy.
4. Honor your father and your mother.
5. You shall not kill.
6. You shall not commit adultery.
7. You shall not steal.
8. You shall not bear false witness against your neighbor.
9. You shall not covet your neighbor's wife.
10. You shall not covet your neighbor's goods.

Some of the words in the commandments might seem strange, but let us look more closely to see how God wants us to live so that we might be happy.

In its longer form in the Bible, the first commandment tells us why we should worship God. We hear again the wonderful things God has done for the people when he rescued them from the slavery of Egypt. Because God has rescued the people, we should believe in him and trust him above all things.

In Israel (which is the name God called his people) the first commandment was the heart of the whole Law, the most important part. When Jesus told a young man that he should love the Lord God above everything else in this world, he was agreeing with this commandment. If we can follow this commandment alone, we are well on our way toward the happiness God promises us.

The second commandment asks us not to take the Lord's name in vain. This is strange language, but it means that we should be serious about God's love for us. It is important that we do not forget about God and his love for us as we become wound up in our own lives and concerns. Like Abraham and Moses, we should entrust all our lives to the Lord and look to the Lord for guidance in all that we do.

The third commandment asks us to set aside one day each week for prayer and relaxation. We dedicate that day to God. As Christians we celebrate Sunday, the day of Jesus' rising from the dead, as our day of prayer. On that day we gather together to give thanks to God in the Eucharist. We give thanks for all God has given us, and we ask for his guidance in our life. This is also a day when we rest from our work, for we are no longer slaves. Now we can take time off in order to enjoy the beautiful life God has given us.

The fourth commandment asks us to respect and honor our father and mother. They have given birth to us and raised us in their love. When we return their love we bring them great happiness, and we help to make our home a wonderful place in which we can live, grow, and enjoy each other.

The remaining commandments teach us how we might live together as a community. As long as we fear that our neighbor will kill us, cheat us, or steal from us, we cannot live in the trust that is necessary for us to be happy. Israel and Jesus took these last six commandments and combined them into one: love one's neighbor as oneself. If we could all live this way, we would create a wonderful community in which we could know one another better and grow in the knowledge and love of God.

who continues to love us in spite of all our weakness

Although these commandments seem reasonable and fairly easy to obey, the truth is that Israel, and indeed all of us, have had a difficult time living up to them. Once the people found their own land and became a nation, Israel became just as sinful as the

Egyptians had been. A few people grew wealthy and powerful. They controlled the country and gathered power around themselves while most of the people were kept poor and at the mercy of the rulers and the rich.

Israel also fell into thinking that since God had chosen her, led her to freedom, and given her land, she was really special. She mistakenly came to think that God loved her, but did not love any other people. God had hoped that Israel would be a sign to the other nations of how to live in peace and happiness. Yes, he did love Israel, but that didn't mean he hated other nations. Again and again, God tried to convince Israel to be a light for the other nations, but Israel didn't listen. She assumed God loved only her, and she became proud. She felt she could do nothing wrong because God was on her side.

Many times God sent prophets to Israel to remind her of God's love and to try to recall her to the Law. "Don't you realize what you are doing when you cheat one another and oppress the poor?" asked the prophets. "You are acting just as the Egyptians did. You have made slaves of your own brothers and sisters. You cheat them of their food and their land. You steal from them the little they need in order to live decently. You do not really love and trust God. You say that you do, but your actions speak differently. If you continue to live this way, Israel will be destroyed, just as Egypt was, and God will not come again to save you."

But the rich and powerful of Israel did not listen

to the prophets. Why should they? Who were these nasty prophets anyway? Who gave them the right to tell Israel what to do? Things were going well. They had a king to rule, protect, and lead them in battle. They had built God a magnificent and beautiful temple. They were careful to worship God with the right sacrifices. They had proven that they were just as good as any other nation; indeed, better, because God loved them above all.

Israel was partly right. God did love her, in spite of all her thirst for wealth and power, in spite of the terrible things she did to her own poor. But God's heart went out to the poor, the hungry, and the powerless. He loved those few people who followed his Law, kept the commandments, and lived as he had shown them.

God suffered because of his love for Israel. He knew that Israel did not truly love him, but he could not stop his own love. Israel's heartlessness pained God. He told the prophets how he suffered because of it. He told them how his love could never die, no matter what Israel did to destroy it. God wanted only to help Israel, to save her from destroying herself, but she wouldn't listen. Destruction was coming down the road. God saw it, the prophets spoke of it, but few in Israel paid any attention.

who is God not only of Israel but of all peoples

God did love Israel, but Israel assumed that he loved no one else. She thought she was special and that God would protect her no matter what happened. It was hard to convince her of God's love for all people. There is a story about a prophet named Jonah which shows us just how hard a task God had in teaching Israel about his love for other peoples.

God asked Jonah to go to the people of Nineveh, for he wanted Jonah to preach to them about the Law. Hopefully they would see how they were living, change their ways, and begin to live in peace and harmony.

But Jonah did not want to go to Nineveh. "They aren't our people," he protested. "Why should I go to them? They're not worth it. They wouldn't listen to me anyway. It's a waste of time."

"They are my people," said God. "I love them as well. I want them to stop hurting one another so that they, too, might find peace and joy."

Jonah was not easy to convince. He simply would not go, so God had to use some harsh tactics to change his mind. To escape God's demands, Jonah decided to take a voyage on a ship. When the ship was at sea a great storm arose, and the sailors were terrified.

As the storm raged around them, Jonah sensed what the problem was, and he began to feel responsible for risking the lives of all the people on board. He knew he was trying to avoid doing what God wanted. The sailors soon realized that the problem was Jonah, and there was only one thing for them to do. They had to throw him overboard in hope that the storm would stop. As soon as they ditched Jonah into the sea, the storm ceased.

A huge fish came along and swallowed Jonah whole. God gave Jonah time to think about things in the belly of that fish. To be exact, he gave him three days.

And Jonah did think. After all, there wasn't much else he could do. Maybe I'd better do what God wants, thought Jonah. He seems pretty determined, sending first the storm and then the fish. All right, Lord. If you get me out of this alive, I'll do what you ask.

On the third day, the fish swam ashore and belched up Jonah, who was thankful to have his feet on dry land again. True to his promise, and perhaps a little fearful of what might happen if he weren't, Jonah set off for Nineveh.

There he preached to the people. He pointed out what they were doing to one another, and he called on them to turn away from their sins and follow the Law of God. No one was more surprised than Jonah when the people of Nineveh not only listened to him, but did what the Lord asked.

"That's more than many of my own people would do, and they should know better," remarked Jonah. Then he gave thanks to God for God's great love for all people.

When we say that God loves us in a special way, we do not mean that he doesn't love other people. Rather, we believe that he has chosen us to be a sign of his wonderful love. If we are signs of God's love, then other people may come to know about him and love him because of us. For he is the God not only of us, but of all the world and its creatures.

Father Almighty

As we discover how much God loves and cares for us, we begin to realize how close he is, and we in turn feel close to him. He is not so different or strange. He is really a person like us who wants to be called by a special name. It is not something lofty or secret, simply the lovely name of Father.

God loves and cares for us as a father does his children. He wants us to be happy and hopes we will be able to enjoy life and grow in love. He is concerned that we have food to eat and freedom to grow, and that we understand his love and learn to love him and all our brothers and sisters in return.

The greatest king in Israel was David, but long before he was a king, David was a poor shepherd boy. While he was in the fields with his sheep, David would sing to God. In one of his greatest songs he called God a shepherd and described how God feeds and cares for his sheep, guiding them to the best pastures so that they might eat, protecting them from wolves, providing them with whatever they need. Following is David's song to God, and we can make it our own prayer:

> The Lord is my shepherd,
>   there is nothing that I need.
> He lets me rest in green pastures;
>   he guides me by restful waters;
>   he refreshes my spirit.
> He leads me along the right paths
>   for he is good and loves me.
> I will trust him and fear nothing,
>   even when I walk in the darkness.
> For you are at my side with your staff
>   and your guidance
>   to give me courage.
> You place good food on a table before me
>   right in the sight of my enemies;
> You pour oil upon my head to cool me;
>   my cup overflows with refreshing drink.
> Only goodness and kindness will follow me
>   all the days of my life,
> And I will live in the Lord's house
>   all of my life.

Maker of Heaven and Earth

God loves everyone and everything because he made us all—from the tiniest atom to the largest galaxy. God made everything that exists. And the entire universe continues from day to day, from moment to moment, only because God loves us, wants us to exist, and therefore holds everything in existence.

The first story in the Bible tells us that in the beginning there was only God. Then, out of his love, he decided to create the world. "Let there be light," he said, and no sooner was the word spoken than it was done. There was light where once there had been only darkness. God separated the light from the darkness, calling the light *day* and the darkness *night*. God saw that what he made was good, and this was the first day of creation.

On each succeeding day, God made new creatures. He made the sun, the moon, and the stars. He made the waters and the sky. He made the plants and the fish, the birds and all the other animals. Since God made them out of his love, they were all good and beautiful, just as God is good and beautiful.

On the sixth day of creation something special happened, for that was when God created human beings. Why are human beings so special? How are we different from the other animals, or from the plants and the planets for that matter? We are different because God created us in his own image. We are the only creatures who are really like God. We can think and talk, laugh and cry, look forward to our future, and remember our past.

Because we are made in his image, God made us the guardians of all his other creatures. It is our joy to look after and care for this wonderful creation. We can use it for our enjoyment, but God also asks that we take care of his beloved creation. We must not abuse our world, for it belongs to God and he loves it very much. We should be careful that we do not destroy it needlessly. It is all right for us to kill animals and plants so that we might eat and live, but when we kill and destroy simply for the joy of killing, we are no longer stewards—we are exploiters. We are then using other creatures selfishly and hurting the earth God loves so much.

Not only did God create everything in the universe at that time so long ago when time first began, but it is God's constant love this very instant that keeps everything in existence. If God were to forget anything he has created, even for the moment it takes to wink, then that thing, no matter how tiny, as tiny as an atom, no matter how huge, as huge as a galaxy, would disappear. It would cease to exist. We are astounded when we realize that God knows and loves each of us individually and that he also loves everything he has made, down to the smallest ant.

We give God our Father thanks for his great love. We thank him for the beautiful universe he has created. We thank him that he has chosen us to be his people, his sign on earth. We thank him for the Law he gave to show us how to live together in peace and happiness. And we thank him for his love for the poor and the enslaved; for this love has, again and again, freed us and brought us into the light of his goodness.

3.
We Believe in Jesus Christ

Jesus is our true teacher about God. He knows how we can be happy. In spite of all the help, including the Law, that our Father has given us, we have seldom been really happy. Something always seems to have gone wrong. Many times we seek things we think will make us happy, but it turns out that they do not.

Jesus is concerned about our happiness. At the very beginning of his ministry, when he spoke to the people on the mountain, he taught nine ways in which we can find real happiness, and we call these nine keys to happiness the Beatitudes.

When we read the Beatitudes, they might seem strange and puzzling. It might be difficult to understand how we can be happy if we are in sorrow, or if we are persecuted. But many women and men have taken these words of Jesus seriously and have found happiness. We call these people saints, and we learn from their lives how they found the happiness Jesus promises all of us.

Following are Jesus' nine keys to happiness:

Happy are the poor in spirit; the kingdom of God belongs to them.

Happy are those who sorrow; they shall be comforted.

Happy are those who are patient; they shall inherit the earth.

Happy are those who hunger and thirst after holiness; they shall be satisfied.

Happy are the merciful; they shall be shown mercy.

Happy are the pure in heart; they shall see God.

Happy are the peacemakers; they shall be called God's children.

Happy are those persecuted for the cause of right; the kingdom of God is theirs.

Happy are you when they insult you and persecute you and say evil things about you because of me; be glad and rejoice, for your reward in the kingdom is great.

What is the kingdom of God Jesus mentions three times in these Beatitudes? Everything Jesus said and did in his life shows us and brings us closer to this kingdom. Jesus told many stories—called parables—and in these stories we can see what the kingdom is like.

The kingdom of God is like a buried treasure, says Jesus. If we were out walking in a field and happened to find a buried treasure, we would quickly bury it again so that no one else would find it. Then we would run home, gather all our belongings, and rush to sell them so that we would have enough money to buy the field. No matter how much the field cost, we would think we were rich because we would soon own the treasure.

When we hear this story we realize how exciting it would be if we could find the kingdom of God in our own lives. If we discovered the kingdom, we would be willing to give up all sorts of things we consider valuable, just so that we might have the kingdom.

If we could believe what Jesus says, wouldn't we begin to seek the kingdom right now? But how would we ever find it? It isn't that easy to find buried treasure. We might search all our lives and never discover it.

But Jesus tells us another story. The kingdom of God is like a merchant, he says. This merchant was always looking around for pearls to buy and then sell again. One day the merchant found a pearl that was worth more than any other pearl in the whole world. Being a lover of pearls and knowledgeable about them, the merchant knew that this pearl was one in a million. Quickly he ran home and put everything he had up for sale so that he could get enough money to buy the pearl. What difference did it make if he sold everything he had? As long as he could get that rare pearl, he would be richer than he could ever think of being without it.

This story might seem to be the same as the first story. Only the names have been changed. But Jesus is a careful storyteller. Each thing he says gives us a clue to the kingdom of God, so we must pay close attention to his words. In the first story, the kingdom of God is the buried treasure we set out to find. But in the second story Jesus tells us that the kingdom of God is like the merchant, not the pearl.

Then who is the pearl? We are. This means that the kingdom of God is searching for us just as hard, perhaps even harder, than we are seeking it.

Many of Jesus' stories tell us how much God loves us and wishes us to be happy by finding the kingdom. As David sang a song about God as a shepherd, Jesus also speaks of God as a shepherd.

Once a shepherd was tending his flock in the fields, and one of the sheep wandered off and lost its way. The shepherd did not discover until evening what had happened, and then he went out to search for the missing sheep.

The shepherd might have thought there was nothing he could do about the lost sheep, but this shepherd could not let the sheep go. He left the rest of the flock in the pasture while he searched through the forest until he finally found the sheep. He picked it up in his arms, carried it on his shoulders and sang all the way back to the flock because he had found this one, lost sheep. This story shows us just how much God loves us and wants us to enjoy the kingdom he has made for us.

who forgives our sins and heals our bodies

Jesus did a great deal more than tell stories about the kingdom of God. He did things for people, and he was able to bring them, then and there, into the kingdom. Jesus taught that in the kingdom all the wrong things we have done, all our sins, are forgiven. No one holds grudges in the kingdom; there is no chance we won't be forgiven.

Jesus never avoided people whom others regard as sinners. He didn't scold them or speak against them. Instead he talked with them, went to their houses to eat and stay, and forgave whatever wrong they had done. Amazingly, when Jesus acted this way with people, they stopped their wrongdoing. They no longer lived as they did before. Jesus changed their lives and they began to live in the kingdom of happiness.

In Jesus' time, there was a man named Zacchaeus who was hated by everyone in the town of Jericho because he collected taxes for the Romans. The Israelites did not like the Romans. They were conquerors and the Jews did not like living under a foreign power. The Romans made the Jews pay taxes, and they used Jews as tax collectors, but did not pay them. So a tax collector was seen as a friend of the enemy, and in addition, in order to make his own living he had to cheat by charging people more money than they really owed. A job like that usually attracted pretty bad characters who were quite comfortable cheating and stealing. Zacchaeus was no exception, and he didn't have a friend in the whole town.

When Zacchaeus heard that Jesus was coming to town he was curious to meet him. After all, he too had heard strange stories about how Jesus taught and how he worked wonders. Zacchaeus also knew that he wouldn't be welcome in the town square, so early on the day Jesus was due to arrive, Zacchaeus hid himself in a tree near the roadside. There he would be able to get a good look at Jesus but could remain hidden from the townspeople.

Jesus was not easily fooled. He looked up into the tree and said, "Zacchaeus, come down from the tree. I want to eat with you and stay at your house tonight."

What was Zacchaeus to do? He had been discovered. Not only that, Jesus knew his name. How could it be? To top it off, Jesus wanted to eat with him and stay with him. Few people in town would even talk to him. People went out of their way to avoid him. Now this great teacher wanted to be his friend.

When Zacchaeus crawled down from the tree and approached Jesus, he saw no hatred in Jesus' eyes. Jesus knew exactly who Zacchaeus was and what he did, yet he greeted Zacchaeus with love and forgiveness. Before Zacchaeus knew what was happening, he found himself saying, "I want to give half of everything I own to the poor."

What was he doing? How ridiculous! No one in his right mind would say such a thing, Yet Zacchaeus intended to go through with it. He didn't regret his words at all. In fact, he was happier than he had ever been in his life.

Jesus looked around at Zacchaeus's neighbors. They too were astounded at what stingy old Zacchaeus had said. This wasn't the cheating tax collector they had known. Jesus said to the people, "Today Zacchaeus has entered the kingdom of God. See how wonderfully happy it has made him."

Jesus had the remarkable power to change people's lives with just a word, a touch, a glance. He never condemned: he forgave. And once people had been forgiven by Jesus, they were not the same as they had been before. Their whole lives changed, and they found the happiness Jesus had promised in the nine Beatitudes.

Jesus often did more than forgive people. Wherever he went, the deaf, the blind, the lame, and the lepers went out to meet him. Jesus' heart opened to these poor people and he healed them. He taught that in the kingdom of his Father there would be no more sickness or pain and every tear would be wiped away. It is easy to see why the first Christians called the entire life of Jesus the Good News. It was not only what he taught, it was also how he acted and lived. "Good News" is the meaning of our word *Gospel*. And the Good News is Jesus himself.

His Only Son

The people Jesus spoke to knew that God was their Father, but God seemed so powerful and distant that it was hard to think of him as a father. Or, if he was a father, he was one to be feared.

Jesus encouraged us to get to know our heavenly Father. He told us not to be afraid. It was all right to call God by names we used for our own fathers when we were children. "Call God Daddy," Jesus advised, "for your heavenly Father is even more loving and caring than our earthly fathers. What earthly father would give his children a stone when they were hungry and asking for bread? No father would do that. Yet earthly fathers sometimes find it hard to be really loving. Your heavenly Father loves you completely all the time. He knows exactly what you need, and he wants to give it to you if you will only ask him."

Jesus understands our heavenly Father so well because he is his Son. He knows the Father better than any other human being. Many times he tells us that he lives only to show us our Father and to bring us back to him. "I want my Father to be your Father as well," he tells us.

He teaches us how to speak to our Father, what we should ask for, and how we might live. We call this beautiful teaching the Lord's Prayer. We use its words often as our own prayer to our Father, and we can also use it as a guide to creating our own prayers with our own words. Jesus invites us to speak continually to this wonderful Father who cares for us and welcomes us into the happiness of his kingdom.

Here is the prayer that Jesus taught us:

> Our Father
> who art in heaven
> hallowed be thy name.
> Thy kingdom come,
> thy will be done
>   on earth as it is in heaven.
> Give us this day our daily bread,
> and forgive us our trespasses
>   as we forgive those who trespass
>   against us.
> And lead us not into temptation
>   but deliver us from evil.

Early Christians concluded this prayer with a little phrase that praised God and thanked him for all he has given us. We still pray this ending during the Eucharist when we pray, "For yours is the kingdom, and the power, and the glory forever."

As they spent more and more time with Jesus, the disciples began to realize that there was something truly special about him. He was a great teacher, but he was more than that. He was more than a marvelous healer, more than even a prophet, as in days gone by.

Israel lies next to the Mediterranean Sea, and storms that begin at sea sweep inland to Israel. The thunderclouds gather and pile on top of one another. The wind blows these huge clouds landward, and the force makes even the great cypress trees of Lebanon shake and bend. The Israelites had always pictured God as riding these mighty and fearful storms, and the storm became a sign for the Jews of God's awesome power.

One day, in order to be alone with Jesus, the disciples went out in a boat on the Sea of Galilee. One of these storms arose, and the waves crashed and the wind howled. The disciples had been napping, but they soon awoke, and when they realized that Jesus was not with them in the boat, they became frightened. Where was he? What would happen to them in this fierce storm?

Then a wonderful thing happened. They saw Jesus walking toward them over the waters. "Do not be afraid," he comforted them, "it is all right," and as he spoke the storm died down.

Who was this man who could control even the

mighty storms? Only God himself could do that. Now they had witnessed that same power in Jesus. He must indeed be God's son.

Our Lord

Using the words of Isaiah, a prophet in Israel's past, Jesus described himself and his mission. His disciples heard Isaiah's words, with which they were familiar, and they felt that the prophecies were coming true. No longer were the prophet's words predicting something that would happen in the future. These wonderful things were happening right now. The old words of Isaiah were coming alive in Jesus:

> The spirit of the Lord has come upon me
> and he has anointed me.
> He sends me to bring good news to the poor,
> and to set free those who are slaves,
> to give sight to the blind
> and to free the prisoners.
> To proclaim a year of favor from the Lord.

During the three years they spent with Jesus, the disciples heard him speak of his Father's kingdom. They had seen sinners and sick people made free to enter that kingdom. They had seen in Jesus power that they thought possible in God alone. Living with Jesus, they felt the beauty and peace of the kingdom.

Then something even more marvelous happened to three of the disciples. Jesus took Peter, James, and John with him up onto a high mountain. There, the disciples saw Jesus surrounded by a brilliant white light. It seemed as though he were clothed with the sun, so brightly did he and his clothes shine.

Then the disciples saw two other people standing with Jesus. One was Moses, who had first met God in the burning bush and then led God's people to freedom out of Egypt. The other person was Elijah, who had been the greatest prophet in Israel. Both men, the greatest heroes of Israel, were pointing to Jesus. He was even greater than they.

Peter, James, and John now knew that all the things they had been thinking and hoping about Jesus were true. He was indeed God's beloved Son. His kingdom was the one that had been promised ever since God had told Moses he would lead the people to freedom. Jesus was the person all the prophets had seen coming to fulfill the hopes and dreams of Israel.

These three men now recognized Jesus not only as a great teacher, but as *the* teacher. All the truths other teachers had taught were to be found in Jesus. The disciples began to realize that Jesus was not just someone who spoke of the kingdom of God: he *was* the kingdom of his Father. Now they knew why all those people—Zacchaeus, the blind, the deaf, the lepers—were able to enter the kingdom simply by meeting Jesus. Now they knew why they themselves felt so joyful whenever they were near him.

Peter, James, and John recognized Jesus as their Lord. They were willing to give him the power to control their lives and even their thoughts. They knew that Jesus alone could bring them perfect peace and happiness. They knew they walked with the man who was making true all the dreams of Israel.

Yet what did Jesus tell them as they came down from the mountain that day? What did this man who held the key to happiness in his word, his glance, his touch, intend to do now? Surely he would bring the kingdom of his Father out into the open where all could see and enter it. He would replace the unhappy world we suffer through with the gloriousness of his Father's kingdom, where every tear would be wiped away and all would be well.

But the man they called Lord told them that they were going to the city of Jerusalem, and that there he would be put to death. Once more the disciples were stunned. Nothing made sense. What kind of Lord was this man anyway?

Conceived of the Holy Spirit

To help us understand more deeply who Jesus was, let us go back to some stories about how he was born. Perhaps we can better understand who he is if we know where he comes from.

who announced the Good News to Mary

We can begin to see that the real story of our life with God is a love story, and as in all love stories, we begin with two people falling in love. They meet each other, and suddenly life is more exciting and richer than it was before.

Then, in most love stories, something happens. The lovers are separated, not permitted to be together, or they feel they do not love each other anymore. We suffer with them as they try to join once again in love.

In the stories we like best, the ones that make us feel full of joy, the two lovers overcome all the barriers that separate them. They find each other and their love again. And that is the end of the story—except for the magical final line. They lived happily ever after.

We could tell the story of God's life with us in the same way. It too is a love story. Our Father created this world, and because he is goodness itself, the world is good. But it is more than good. For God created us because of his love. And his love, which we call the Holy Spirit, couldn't help but create a universe with all the wonder, beauty, and truth of God himself. Of all the things in the universe, God especially loves us because we are created in his image. We are like him.

However, as in most love stories, something went wrong. We fell out of love with God. We forgot about him. We wanted to do things our own way, and we didn't care that much about God's love for us. We began to do things on our own, without thinking about God, and pretty soon we began to feel unhappy and miserable.

Even though we had forgotten him, our Father did not stop loving us. He was still hopelessly in love, but he knew he couldn't force us to love him. He had to try to win us back, to make us fall in love with him all over again.

So he began searching for a way that he might come together with us again. When he spoke to Moses and promised to lead the slaves out of Egypt, he was trying to win us over to his love. God was true to his promises, but, as we have seen, Israel was not won over. She wasn't ready to love him in return and keep the Law he gave her.

It made no difference. Whether she loved him or not, God was head over heels in love with Israel. In his eyes, the sun rose and set over his beloved. When Israel refused to follow the Law that would bring her happiness, God's heart ached. He told the prophets how he suffered each time Israel mistreated her poor or failed to live in peace. Even though he failed with each attempt to win Israel back, God still lived in the hope that someday they might join together again in love.

Finally, God had an idea. What if he sent his Son to live as one of us? That Son might be able to lead us back to happiness. Unfortunately, it wasn't as simple as that. Being in love, God knew that he couldn't win us back against our will. It was necessary that human beings freely invite God into their lives. So God had to find someone who would totally respond to his love and thereby make a place for his Son to come into the world.

In a young woman named Mary, God found such a person. In her, God saw all that was lovely and beautiful in Israel. And Mary was able to love God in return. God hoped she would welcome his Son and give him a place in the world.

One day God's messenger, Gabriel, appeared to Mary as she was sitting in her garden. "Hail Mary, full of grace," the angel said in greeting. "God has chosen you among all women to be the mother of his Son. You will give birth to the savior Israel has been waiting for all these hundreds of years."

Mary was not yet married, and she did not understand how this wonderful thing could happen, but she consented to God's plan. She opened her heart in love and invited God to become flesh in her body.

If it had not been for Mary's openness, Jesus could not have been born into the world.

God respects our freedom and our will. He will not impose his way on us, for if he forced us to love him, he knows it would not really be love. Love must be freely given. On behalf of Israel, and indeed of all people, Mary freely responded to our Father's love by becoming the mother of the savior, the mother of Jesus. Because she responded so fully to the Father, to this day she is called the happiest among women.

and Mary joyfully carried the Good News to her cousin Elizabeth

When Mary received the angel's message and agreed to become the mother of the savior, a new age came into being. Something was to happen in Israel that had never happened before.

Yet there were certain signs that the birth of Jesus would not be entirely new and strange. As Father Abraham was given a son in his old age so that his descendants would be as numerous as the sands, Mary's cousin Elizabeth, an old woman who had been unable to have children, became pregnant. She and her husband, Zachary, would be the parents of John, who would announce the coming of Jesus. God was at work again.

When Mary found out about the Good News of the coming savior, she immediately went to visit her cousin. And when Elizabeth saw Mary coming, the child leaped within her: he already recognized his savior. Elizabeth greeted her cousin, saying, "Blessed are you among women, and blessed is the fruit of your womb." Elizabeth knew now that a time was coming when every tear would be wiped away and joy would reign.

Today we still honor Mary as did the Angel Gabriel and Elizabeth. We ask Mary, as the woman God loved above all, to pray for us in our own times of trouble, to be with us in the hour of death. Following are the words we use to honor this maiden who is the mother of our Lord:

> Hail Mary,
> full of grace.
> The Lord is with you.
> Blessed are you among women,
>   and blessed is the fruit of your
>   womb, Jesus.
> Holy Mary,
> Mother of God,
> pray for us sinners now
>   and at the hour of our death.

When Elizabeth's son, John, grew up, he began to preach to the people. "Turn back from your sins," he cried out. "Return to the Lord. Be baptized so that your sins might be no more." Because of what he preached, John was called the Baptist.

When the people saw John they were surprised, for he sounded and acted like one of the prophets. Some thought he was Elijah come back to life, for they believed this would happen just before the world ended. Others argued that John could not possibly be a prophet, for no prophets had appeared for hundreds of years. The time of prophets was over. Yet John spoke and acted like a prophet, and he told the people that soon a saviour would appear to them.

Something new was about to happen in Jesus, something that had never happened before. Yet this was the same God we have come to know in Israel's history. The God who gave a child to Abraham and Sarah in their old age also gave a son to Elizabeth and Zachary in theirs. This is the God who spoke to Israel through the prophets. He spoke then of his great love, of his hope that one day Israel might return that love and live in the peace and happiness of his Law. Now God spoke again through his prophet, John. "Soon God himself will show us his love; soon the day he has promised in the prophets will come upon the earth," said John.

And Was Born of the Virgin Mary

y was married to Joseph, her fiancé. Because the Romans demanded that everyone return to their birthplace to be taxed, Joseph had to journey back to his own birthplace in Bethlehem just before it was time for Mary's child to be born. While Joseph and Mary were away from Nazareth, Jesus was born.

in a stable in Bethlehem

We can see that Jesus is the Son of Israel's God by the way in which he was born. Long ago God had told Moses that he was on the side of those who were enslaved, suffering, and poor. He was not at home in the marble palaces of kings, but in the shabby huts of slaves. And when it came time for Jesus to be born, it was not in the comfort of a home. He was born in a poor stable because there was no room for Mary and Joseph at the inn. Where else should the God who once freed the slaves be born?

Israel's greatest king was not born a king at all: David had been a poor shepherd who sang songs praising God as he watched his flock in the fields. So, the Son of God who was Israel's true king was not born among riches, but among simple shepherds. That night, only poor shepherds greeted God's coming into this world. They left their sheep and traveled that night to Bethlehem to see him there.

and in fulfillment of the Law and prophets

When a king is born in a stable, there is bound to be some difficulty recognizing him, and Jesus was often unrecognized during his life. He was a king who did not look like one. The people of Israel expected certain things of a savior. They had many ideas about what he would be like and what he would do. How would they recognize a savior if he did not meet these expectations?

After his birth, Mary and Joseph took Jesus to the temple to be dedicated to God, for the Law demanded that the first son of each family belong to God. As good Jews, Mary and Joseph followed and obeyed this Law.

In the temple at this time was an old man named Simeon who had been promised that he would not die before he had seen the savior of Israel with his own eyes. Simeon, who was very old and could not live much longer, was worried that he wouldn't live to see the savior. And Simeon also wondered how he would recognize him if he did see him.

On this day, as Simeon entered the temple and saw Mary and Joseph with the baby Jesus, he knew immediately that this was the boy who was to be the savior of Israel. Simeon's and Israel's hopes had been answered. Simeon eagerly took the child into his arms and prayed the following beautiful prayer. From that day on, many Christians have prayed it each night before they go to bed:

Now, all powerful Master,
> you allow your servant to depart in peace;
> for you have been faithful to your promise.
> My eyes have seen your saving action
> which you have shown to all the peoples:
> A light to guide the nations
> and give glory to Israel, your people.

Then Simeon turned to Mary and said, "This child is going to be a sign of contradiction. It will be hard for many people to see that he is indeed the savior. Some people will be against him and try to destroy him, and your own heart will be broken."

Our love story is far from over. God has once more made contact with us whom he loves. But even though we have been prepared for this day by all the Law and by the prophets, will we be able to recognize that love? How far we are from real peace and happiness when we cannot recognize Jesus as the one who can give us the happiness we want so much!

He Suffered Under Pontius Pilate

When Jesus grew up, he taught that in his Father's kingdom there was no such thing as fear. Fear is created by the world to keep us from being happy.

But it was very hard for the disciples to believe that Jesus was right about fear. After all, everyone feels there are many things to be afraid of in this world. We would like to believe what Jesus says, but our fear stops us short.

Jesus must have become discouraged. How could he bring his disciples into the kingdom unless he could convince them that their fears were groundless? There was no reason to be afraid: God would save them and make all well in his kingdom. But nothing Jesus could say seemed to convince them completely, for they held onto their fear.

Then Jesus realized that the reason we are slaves of fear is because we are terrified of death. That is the real trouble. We know that sooner or later we are going to die. And the fear of death prevents us from entering God's kingdom and enjoying our life in happiness.

Jesus said to the disciples, "There's nothing to be afraid in death. It cannot really kill you. Death is just the passing over into my Father's kingdom." That might be easy for Jesus to say, but it is hard for us to believe.

Jesus decided that the only way to convince us that he was right about death would be to walk through the experience of death and show us that it can't destroy us. Then he told his disciples just what he intended to do. "We're going to go to Jerusalem, and there I will be handed over to the government and put to death."

"But, Lord, you're crazy to think of doing that," said Simon Peter, who was always the first to react to anything. "Why would you want to do such a thing?"

"Quiet, Peter," scolded Jesus. "You're acting just as the world acts instead of as I have taught you. Don't you believe in the kingdom yet?"

in agony in the garden

Jesus and his disciples set off for Jerusalem where he would show them how to walk through the powers of sin and death. On the night he knew that one of his disciples, named Judas, would betray him, he took the disciples to the Garden of Gethsemane.

Jesus was human just as we are. He had never died before. How could he be absolutely sure that what he taught about death was true? Now he found himself a few hours away from painful suffering, and he was frightened. He needed to feel his friends close to him for strength and support. He wanted to find assurance from his Father for what he was about to do.

Jesus took his three closest disciples with him into

the garden to pray, but as usual the disciples didn't understand what was happening. So many things had occurred, in those last few days that it was hard for them to understand. Jesus kept talking about his coming death and betrayal, but only a few days ago half the people of Jerusalem had greeted him as their king and savior. What was going on anyway?

It was very late at night. Perhaps if they could catch a few moments of sleep . . . So Peter, James, and John took care of their troubles by sleeping while Jesus, left all alone, prayed to his Father.

Jesus was terrified about what would happen to him. He asked his Father to give him some other course of action. Yet in the end he agreed to do his Father's will, no matter what it might cost. Throughout this night of horrible waiting, Jesus realized how alone he was.

Not once but three times he found his best friends asleep. He asked his Father to save him from what would happen, and his prayer was greeted only with silence.

By the end of the waiting, as he heard the soldiers approach, Jesus knew there was no way out but to walk through death and face all its terrors. Finally, Judas arrived with the authorities. Jesus was arrested, and the disciples fled from him in horror and fear. The suffering of Jesus' Passion had begun.

in the scourging with whips

Throughout the night, his enemies dragged Jesus back and forth from trial to trial. Finally he was whipped brutally. Jesus did not suffer more than many others have suffered throughout the ages, but neither was his pain less frightening and terrible.

Some people may experience more pain than did Jesus, and some may feel much less, but, being human, we know there is a good chance each one of us will suffer in some way. In the midst of our suffering, we cry out, and all the things we take for granted and find easy to believe at happier times seem insignificant and even ridiculous in the face of our pain.

In the Beatitudes, Jesus taught us about real happiness. As he felt the whip tear at his flesh, he cried out at the pain those Beatitudes might save us from. Yet in spite of his suffering, Jesus didn't give up hope. He still believed there was a way through the suffering to the happiness of the kingdom of God. Pain and suffering did not kill that dream for Jesus. Even then he believed that the kingdom of his loving Father was more real than the stabs of pain crashing through his body.

as he is crowned with thorns

Then, even greater suffering was inflicted on Jesus. His one dream was of his Father's kingdom. If people could give up their worldly ways and learn to think in the new and wonderful ways of God's kingdom, all his suffering would be worth the price. But Jesus' dream was mocked, misunderstood, and rejected.

Jesus never had any intention of becoming a king. Kings belonged to the world. In his Father's kingdom there were no kings other than the Father, yet people hadn't even understood that much of Jesus' dream. They thought he wanted to be a king himself. Pilate, the Roman governor, was afraid that Jesus might start a revolution and seize power. His own people did not understand him, and they wanted no part of God's wonderful kingdom. "We're quite happy with the way things are," they yelled. "We have no king but Caesar."

As they put the prickly crown of thorns on his head, Jesus understood that his death might be senseless. He had hoped that if he could walk through death his followers might be able to give up their fear and enter the kingdom. But he saw that he had been misunderstood. His death might accomplish nothing. These people—who a few days ago had welcomed him—now rejected him. His own followers fled from him and went back home.

We can endure enormous pain as long as we believe it means something, but when the suffering becomes meaningless and useless, it is much harder to bear.

as he is made to carry his own cross

Jesus taught that it is our own sin, our wrong way of thinking and acting, that finally brings about our death. Whenever we refuse to forgive one another, we lock ourselves more and more into a way of thinking and living that eventually destroys us. This happens when we judge others, hold grudges, are envious or refuse to love. All of these sins create a cross that we must carry and upon which we shall eventually die.

But what about Jesus? He did not enter into these false ways of thinking and living. In his whole life he never refused to forgive anyone. Indeed, his readiness to forgive people was scandalous to the authorities. Many times people brought sinners to Jesus so that he could judge them, yet never once did he condemn a sinner. He would turn to the accusers and bring their own secret sins into the harsh light of judgment. Even then, he judged not to condemn but to help them see their situation and leave their sins behind.

Jesus had to carry a cross he had no part in creating. His ways of living and thinking should have spared him this cross, but he chose to suffer for us. He died so that we would be free of the sins we have committed.

He took these sins upon himself by taking up his cross. He took up the cross to show he was no one special. He could walk through death just as we can if we completely trust in our Father. We can follow

Jesus through death even though we are laden and burdened by all our wrong ways of thinking and by all the unloving things we have done. Even when we are oppressed and weighed down by all this, Jesus will show us a way to walk through suffering, even through the dark valley of death.

Was Crucified, Dead, and Buried

There was no escape for Jesus. If he were to forge a path through death, he had no choice but to die.

When they came to the place called the Skull, the soldiers nailed Jesus to the cross. There he hung for three hours. In some ways he was lucky, for crucifixion often took days to kill a person. But Jesus was in a weakened condition from the events of recent days, so he suffered only a few hours agony on the cross.

In the midst of this agony, Jesus felt abandoned. He cried out, "My God, my God, why have you forsaken me?" He felt the terrible loneliness, the pain, the senselessness, the lack of concern of the people around him. He tasted death just as we will.

But there was something meaningful and different in Jesus' death. As we have seen, we weave the shape of our death by all of our sinful thought and action. Yet Jesus had not done the same. He freely took our burden of sin upon himself and, by dying, freed us from that slavery.

A beautiful story about Jesus' death helps us understand its meaning more clearly. History tells us that Jesus was crucified at the place of the Skull. But whose skull was it? Legend says the skull is Adam's. He was the first man, and there he was buried.

Adam and his wife, Eve, were the first man and woman. God had placed them in a special garden where they were to care for the garden and the animals. God hoped they would enjoy their life. However, there was one catch: they could not eat of the tree of the knowledge of good and evil.

A serpent tempted Eve to eat the fruit of that tree, and she in turn persuaded Adam to do the same. This was the first example of the wrong thinking and acting that we call sin. God had created us to be happy. Since he created us, he also knew how we might be happy. Yet Adam and Eve chose otherwise, and their choice gave birth to the sin and death that have ruled us ever since. Life as we know it—with all its fear, its war, its hatred, its suffering, and its death—came to be.

This is not the end of the story. There was another tree in the garden as well: the tree of life. When Adam and Eve were driven out of the garden and into the harsh world because of their sin, an angel gave the seeds from the tree of life to Adam's son, Seth. "When your father Adam dies," said the angel, "put these seeds in his throat. From them shall grow a tree that will one day restore all that has been lost to you."

When his father died, Seth did as the angel told him, and from the seeds Seth put in Adam's throat sprouted a tree that began a marvelous journey through our history.

The tree became the staff by which Moses led the Israelites out of Egypt. He stretched forth his staff and the Red Sea parted so that his people could cross over into freedom. After many more centuries, the staff became the rod by which King David ruled over Israel. Finally, the wood became the cross upon which Jesus died.

By eating from the tree of the knowledge of good and evil, Adam and Eve started that thought and action we call sin, which leads to death. By dying on the tree of life, Jesus confirmed his life and teaching as holy. Jesus, in his obedience to God, corrected what Adam had undone. Now, by means of his cross, Jesus leads us through death and into everlasting life.

Jesus won for us what Adam and Eve longed for. He did not restore us to that original Garden of Eden, for we will never lose our knowledge of good and evil. Instead, Jesus gained for us in addition the joy of real life. This story of the tree of life helps us see why Christians say that Jesus saved us by dying on the cross.

Descended into Hell

Our fantastic legend continues after Jesus' death on the cross. In those days, the place of the Skull was thought to be the center of the world. At the time it was believed that anyone who died went to the underworld, where people continued to exist, but not nearly as well as on earth.

When Jesus died, the legend says that his spirit slid down the pole of the cross and right into the underworld. All the people who had ever lived were there, condemned to be there because they did not know how to enter the kingdom. Jesus spoke to them of the kingdom and freed them to enter it right then.

Through his power alone, Jesus was able to bring people into the kingdom. We have seen him using this power when he was alive. Zacchaeus did nothing except meet Jesus, and he immediately began to think and act in the way of the kingdom rather than the way of the world. Now, in the underworld, Jesus' ability to bring people into the kingdom extended even to those who had lived before his time and knew nothing of his teachings. In Jesus, we see God's love extend all the way to the ends of the earth and all the way back to the beginning of time.

The people Jesus met in the underworld could not enter the kingdom because, like Adam and Eve, they had been enslaved to false ways of thinking. Jesus spoke of these false ways of thinking as the ways of the world. He said that Satan was the prince of this world, and he called Satan the father of lies.

Our legend continues as Jesus entered the underworld where Satan ruled. As with every hero, Jesus must slay the dragon. So he fought a great battle with Satan. What did he use for a weapon? His cross, of course! If the cross is grasped at the top, it can be used as a sword, and with that great sword Jesus subdued Satan. From then on the power of Satan was doomed. Jesus' teaching about his Father's kingdom was bound to win. After all, as we have seen in Jesus' death on the cross, there is really nothing to be afraid of.

The Third Day He Rose Again from the Dead

You might be tempted to ask, What do you mean there is nothing to be afraid of? This whole story is frightening. But we haven't yet heard the whole story. Let us come back from our journey into legends to the real story of Jesus' death.

None of the disciples believed that Jesus escaped death that Friday. He was dead. What more was there to say? Jesus was a failure. All the things he had told them were really too good to be true. It would be wonderful to believe in the kingdom of God. It would be joy supreme if we could let go of our fears, but that just wasn't the case. Jesus was dead, and everything he said about not being afraid of death didn't help. When you're dead, you're dead. And that's the way it is.

This must have been what those first disciples thought as they took Jesus' body down from the cross and placed it in the tomb. There was nothing to do but sneak back home, remember the good times they'd had with Jesus, and perhaps dream of what might have been.

However, three days after his death, strange things began to happen to this group of Jesus' followers. First of all, three women went to his tomb. Jesus had died just before the Jewish Sabbath, and there had been no time to anoint his body for burial. After the Sabbath the three women went to carry out the funeral customs.

When they came to the tomb, they were surprised to see that the stone that covered the entrance had been rolled away, and Jesus' body was gone. The women reported to the other disciples that an angel had told them that Jesus was risen from the dead. If this were true, then everything Jesus had said about death was true. The other disciples weren't ready to believe the women. "They are easily influenced. They'll believe anything," they said.

Throughout the day and those following there were numerous stories that Jesus was not dead. He appeared to some of the disciples as they were on their way to Emmaus. They recognized him when he broke bread with them as he had done in life and as he had asked them to do in memory of him. He also appeared to Simon Peter and other disciples.

Suddenly, these people, broken in spirit a few days before, were bursting with joy. Jesus had been right. The kingdom of God was real and Jesus had shown the way into the kingdom. He even revealed death for what it was: a plot to keep us afraid and chained to our sinful ways. But there was no need for fear. Suddenly these men and women who had felt nothing but fear showed no fear at all. Jesus was alive. He had risen from the dead.

He Ascended into Heaven and Sits at the Right Hand of the Father

During that joyful time after Easter, Jesus often appeared to his disciples. It was a time of great learning for them. All the things Jesus had taught them began to make sense. For the first time they came to see the meaning of Jesus; their eyes were opened to the possibilities of what life could be when you lived as Jesus taught.

The disciples hoped that this time could continue forever. Jesus was no longer among them as he had been, but he was often seen when they gathered to give thanks and break bread together.

However, Jesus knew that if he remained with his disciples they would not come to their full growth. They would always be dependent on him and tied to him. Jesus had come to bring real freedom, and that meant freedom from any imprisonment and dependence, even on Jesus himself.

Toward the end of this Easter time, Jesus began to speak more and more about his coming departure. Such talk naturally upset the disciples. Hadn't they been sad and pained when he died? Must they separate again—this time forever? "We want to be with you always," they pleaded.

But Jesus was firm. "If I do not leave, you will never receive the gift of the Holy Spirit within you. The Spirit will lead you and teach you from now on. Under the Spirit's guidance you will carry the Good News I have told you to the ends of the earth. I have chosen you for a mission. I have shown you the way of life. I have revealed to you the joy that is yours in my Father's kingdom. Now it is up to you to take that Good News out from our small group and carry it wherever you go. The Holy Spirit will lead you on this mission. The Spirit will give you the knowledge you need and comfort you when you feel discouraged and overwhelmed by what you are sent to do."

One day Jesus said farewell to his disciples and disappeared from their sight. Once again they were alone. They stared in wonder, their mouths hanging open, their faces searching the skies. They must have been a sight! A messenger from God asked them, "Why are you looking up into the clouds? As he has promised you, Jesus will return at the end of time to bring in his Father's kingdom."

Confused and stunned, the group made its way

back into the city of Jerusalem where they waited for the gift of the Holy Spirit Jesus had promised them. For nine days and nights they stayed together in the upper room and prayed. What would the future bring? How would they be able to fulfill the task Jesus had given them? Where would they find the courage, the understanding, the power to show the kingdom to others? When would this Spirit come upon them? It was a time of faith, but faith without much knowledge. Other than to remain together and pray, the disciples did not know what to do.

One thing the disciples did know was where Jesus had gone this time. He had returned to his Father. They knew he would bring all their prayers and concerns to the Father on their behalf. All they could do was wait for the moment when the Father would send the Holy Spirit to bring Jesus' mission to its completion.

From There He Shall Come to Judge the Living and the Dead

Jesus had said that the time was near when the power of the kingdom of God would come into the world. Soon it would not be difficult to recognize the kingdom. There would be no further need for secrecy: the kingdom would be neither hard to find nor difficult to enter.

Jesus spoke of a new age when the choice between the way of the world and the way of the kingdom would be clear to all. The world's ways and thoughts would be exposed for the unhappiness they create. Everyone would be able to see the ways of the kingdom and the happiness possible there.

At first the disciples expected this new age to come within their own lifetime. When they saw Jesus rise from the dead, they believed the kingdom would come then. As they gathered in prayer in the upper room, they no doubt expected that in a matter of days, or at most years, the time would be ripe. The world would soon end so that the kingdom could begin to spread its joy through all God's creation.

The disciples knew what would happen on the day when the kingdom came out of hiding and replaced the world. Jesus would return again, but this time it would be impossible to mistake him. During his lifetime, it had not always been easy to recognize Jesus. Many heard what he said and even saw his signs, but they still could not recognize him as the Lord who calls us home to joyful life in his Father's kingdom. It is often hard for us to see the truth in our own life. Life is confusing. There are too many unanswered questions. Jesus did not fit the descriptions of the Messiah the Jewish people were waiting for, so many did not receive him. But when he comes again there will be no difficulty in recognizing him and knowing who he is.

When Jesus returns it will be for one purpose only: to set up the kingdom to replace the world. He will invite into this kingdom all who have longed for it and sought it in their own lives. Some will have already refused the invitation by choosing hatred over love; holding grudges over forgiving; choosing death over life, fear over joy.

When Jesus returns to bring his kingdom into the light, the Last Judgment will occur. At this time all people will come before Jesus, and he will decide whether they are able to enter into the kingdom. All those who have glimpsed the light and tried, however poorly, to live in the manner of the kingdom will be invited in at that time. Those who have rejected the ways of the kingdom—the ways of love—will be refused entrance.

There is another meaning to the Last Judgment. Judgment means separation. In the Last Judgment (for there is never any judgment in the kingdom) the elements of the world within us will be separated from the elements of the kingdom.

No one is perfect. We may want to live in love, but often we fail to be loving. We seem to enjoy hurting others, we are afraid to love and to be loved. In the Last Judgment, all in us that belongs to the world will be separated from the love in us that belongs to the kingdom.

If there is more of the world in us than of the kingdom, this separation might be painful. We may feel as if most of us has been stripped away. At the same time, we will see how stupid it is to be afraid, how ridiculous it is to hold grudges, how jealousy keeps us from the love we want so much. We may experience pain as we are torn from the ways of thinking we have been attached to, but it will be a joyful time as well, since we will finally be free to love as God loves us.

The disciples knew that the stakes were high. Jesus had always told them how important it was to change their way of thinking and living so that they could prepare for the coming of the kingdom, so they could taste the joy of the kingdom now instead of waiting for that far-off day.

As Christians, we believe that the day is coming when the world and its ways will pass away so that the joy of the kingdom can bring all creation home to our Father. Whenever it comes in God's own time, we look forward to that day. Meanwhile, we prepare ourselves by turning away from the world's thoughts of power and selfishness so that we can grow in the love of our Father who wishes to bring us into everlasting happiness.

4.
We Believe in the Holy Spirit

The disciples and friends of Jesus gathered together in the upper room for nine days. They spent this time in prayer, waiting for the promise of Jesus to be fulfilled. How could they know what would happen? Who was this Holy Spirit who would guide them in the truth?

On the ninth day, as they were assembled, the sound of a great rushing wind was heard. The Spirit has often been called the breath of God. Like the wind, it can be felt, although it cannot be seen. Like the wind, no one can predict the Spirit or contain it. It blows where it will.

Suddenly, tongues of flame appeared over the head of each disciple. The prophets had often used the image of fire to describe the Spirit. Moses first met God in the burning bush, and when Moses led the people out of Egypt, God went before them as a pillar of cloud by day and a column of fire by night. The Holy Spirit is the light of God in the world. The Spirit brings our life out of the darkness and into the light.

On Pentecost, which is what we call this day that the Spirit descended upon the disciples, we see the beginning of the final part of Jesus' mission. Throughout his life, Jesus had worked with his disciples. He had carefully taught them about his Father's kingdom, and he had led them to see that kingdom by his signs and miracles. In his Resurrection, he had convinced them of the kingdom's power by destroying the fear of death.

But now Jesus' work on earth was over. By the

guidance of the Holy Spirit, Jesus' followers would carry his Good News to all parts of the world and into every corner of our lives. At first the followers of Jesus were limited to this small group, but today all Christians have the mission Jesus entrusted to his disciples.

We are the salt of the earth who now give life pungency and flavor. We are the light of the world entrusted to bring understanding, truth, forgiveness, and healing into the world. We are the people who have heard the Good News of Jesus and accepted it as the truth. We have been given the wonderful gift of the Holy Spirit who leads us day by day and deepens our appreciation of God's love and goodness.

When the flame of the Holy Spirit descended upon the disciples that first Pentecost, they found themselves speaking in all kinds of languages. At that time in Jerusalem there were people from many different lands, but each person heard the disciples speaking in his or her own native language. Here again was a sign of what was to come. These disciples would never see each other again after that great day. They had come to know and love one another as they had traveled with Jesus over the last few years. They had grown to understand each other's strengths and weaknesses; they had helped and corrected each other.

But now greater things were demanded of them. They were to go out of Jerusalem and out of Israel to the ends of the earth. Jesus depended on them, as he depends on us, to carry his message of the kingdom and of his Father's love to all people. In just a few years, thanks to these disciples, people as far away as Spain and India would hear about this wonderful man, Jesus, and the way of living he spoke of that can bring total happiness.

who spoke through the prophets

Pentecost was not the first time the Holy Spirit had appeared in our lives. Pentecost was the final and greatest outpouring of the Spirit, but the Holy Spirit has been present throughout history. The Holy Spirit spoke through all the prophets of Israel. When it spoke through the mouth of the prophet Amos, the Spirit of goodness and truth asked Israel to stop cheating and oppressing the poor. The same Spirit commanded the prophet Jeremiah to tell Israel that if she did not return to God's Law she would be destroyed. The Spirit allowed the prophet Isaiah to comfort Israel when she was captured and imprisoned in the foreign country of Babylon.

When David was made king over Israel he was anointed with oil, and the Spirit of God was seen in him. When Moses led the people out of Egypt it was the Holy Spirit who gave him the power to convince Pharaoh to let the people go. And at the very beginning of the universe, when God said, "Let there be light," it was the Spirit of God that hovered over the darkness. It was through the Spirit that everything was created. Without the Holy Spirit, nothing would exist. The Spirit of God is as necessary to us as the air we breathe. If we stopped breathing we would soon die, but if God's Spirit were entirely removed from us, we would not exist.

We find God first of all in the Father of Jesus—the Father who created all things, led the people out of slavery, and made them into his special nation of Israel. We find God in Jesus, who calls us into his Father's kingdom. And we find God in the Holy Spirit who leads us back to the Father and is the very air we breathe. We call this experience of God the Trinity, for there are not three gods, but only one. Yet in that one God we experience three persons: the Father, the Son, and the Holy Spirit. We give thanks and praise to our God in a special prayer that honors him. We call this prayer the Doxology, which means a prayer of praise and glory:

> Glory be to the Father, and to the Son,
> and to the Holy Spirit,
> As it was in the beginning,
> is now and ever shall be,
> world without end. Amen.

And in the Holy Catholic Church

When the Holy Spirit descended upon the disciples at Pentecost, the church was born. From then on, the center of the Holy Spirit's activity in the world would be the group of people who heard Jesus and believed in him. We are the church. The church is not the buildings, the priests, the bishops, or the pope. The church is the family of God who knows that God loves us and who tries to live as Jesus taught. In the church, the Spirit of God today finds a dwelling place. From the church, the Good News of Jesus brings light and hope to all the world.

The church is not the kingdom Jesus promised, but it is the place where we can learn about the kingdom. The church is the people who encourage us and help us come closer to the kingdom; it is the place where we work for the kingdom; it is the family of all who want to live the loving way Jesus lived. In the church we can learn how to trust Jesus' vision. In the church we can be nourished in our faith. As the church, our own lives can be signs for others that there is a happier way of living than the way the world recommends.

When we examine the life of Peter, whom Jesus chose to be leader of his church, we see how we can grow by bringing ourselves into the loving family of Jesus and allowing God's Spirit to lead us. Every time we meet Peter, it seems as if he is just as wrong as he is right. If Jesus had wanted his church to be perfect, he would never have allowed Peter into the church, let alone put him in charge of it.

When he made Peter the leader of the church, Jesus was saying clearly that this is not a family where people have to be perfect. Rather, it is a family where we can make mistakes and grow. We belong to the church not because we live in the kingdom but because someday we want to live in the kingdom. The love and guidance we receive from one another in the church can help our hope come true.

One thing we can say about Peter is that he never had any doubt about what he wanted. He believed Jesus when Jesus spoke of the kingdom. Peter wanted to enter that kingdom. He wanted to be like Jesus.

When Peter and the other disciples in the boat saw Jesus walking toward them over the water, Peter shouted, "I want to do that too."

"Come, Peter," Jesus said. Jesus never said that Peter should not try to walk on water, or that he could not. Jesus never claimed that walking on water was something only he could do. Jesus encouraged Peter's desire to walk on water.

Peter scrambled up and stepped off the boat, and he didn't sink! He could actually walk on water! He felt light and was filled with happiness as he moved toward Jesus. Then something happened. Perhaps Peter realized that he didn't know how to walk on water. Perhaps he suddenly lost his confidence, looked down at the waves, and panicked. Just then he began to sink. "Help me, Lord," he cried, and Jesus lifted him up out of the water and took him into the boat.

On another occasion Jesus asked the disciples who they thought he was. Once more it was Peter who was first with an answer. "You are the Christ, the Son of the living God," he exclaimed. Peter was willing to believe and trust in Jesus. It was that faith, that yearning to believe, that Jesus rewarded when he chose Peter as the leader of the church. It certainly wasn't Peter's knowledge or his courage, for right after Jesus selected Peter as leader of the disciples he explained that he had to go to Jerusalem and die. Peter wanted no part of this. "Let's do something else instead," he suggested, and Jesus had to rebuke him. Once more Peter had put his foot in his mouth.

After three years of living and learning with Jesus, Peter and the disciples had not changed that much. Peter was still the same, always promising more than he was able to deliver. On the night he would be betrayed, Jesus told them, "You will all abandon me."

But that is ridiculous, thought Peter. We would never do a thing like that. And again he spoke recklessly.

"Even if everyone else runs away, Lord, I will stick by you."

"Peter, Peter," said Jesus, shaking his head. "Before the rooster crows tomorrow morning, you will deny you even know me—not once but three times."

And of course Jesus was right. Peter, whom Jesus called the Rock, proved the unsteadiest of all.

After the Resurrection, Jesus appeared to Peter again. Peter must have been grief-stricken because he did just what Jesus predicted: he failed his master. He probably expected Jesus to scold him, even reject him as a disciple. But Jesus did not say a word about what happened. Nothing made him change his mind about Peter. For success or failure is not important for Christians. We can afford to fail. We can afford to do the worst things in the world, for we can be forgiven. We are forgiven. And as Peter often did, we can think wrong things. That too can be corrected.

Jesus didn't choose Peter to lead his church because Peter was smart or successful, or even because Peter had faith.

"Do you love me, Peter?" Jesus asked him.

That is the important question. We do not have to be good, or right, or wise. Do we love Jesus? That is the only requirement for belonging to his church. And more that that, will we let Jesus love us?

"Do I love you? Oh, yes, I love you, Lord," Peter replied, looking sheepishly at the ground. He must have wondered if Jesus would mention the matter of his denial. When would he be scolded?

"Feed my sheep," said Jesus.

But what about the horrible thing I did, thought Peter. When will he ask about that?

"Do you love me, Peter?" Jesus asked a second time.

"You know I love you, Lord," replied Peter. "I

don't do the right things. I'm probably the worst choice you could make for a disciple. But, yes, I love you."

"Feed my sheep," said Jesus.

And Peter thought to himself, this time I'll do better. I won't lose heart again. Never again will I deny you, Jesus. Never again will I embarrass you. I'll be good. I'll make it all right. I'll show what a good shepherd I can be. You'll be proud of me.

Again Jesus' words interrupted Peter's dreams for the future. "Do you love me, Peter?"

Finally, Peter realized that love was enough. There is no need to promise what you cannot deliver. There is no need to tell yourself you won't fail again. You may fail again, but that is all right. It is enough to love and to be loved—that alone can work miracles.

"Yes, I love you, Lord," said Peter.

"Feed my sheep," replied Jesus for the third time. And then Peter saw that this was enough.

And it was, for when we see Peter and the other disciples after Pentecost, they are not the same. Not only have they found the words to talk about the kingdom and about Jesus, the disciples themselves have become signs of the Father's kingdom. They heal the lame and the blind just as Jesus did. They forgive sins just as Jesus did. And they still remain disciples, for they forgive and heal not by their own power, but by the name and power of Jesus. They still make mistakes, but it is all right.

At one point, Peter found himself in a bad argument with Paul the apostle. Once again Peter was in the wrong, but it was all right. He stood corrected and he went on.

At the end of his life, Peter was about to be crucified just as Jesus had been. Years before, Peter had denied he knew Jesus because he was afraid of what might happen to him. But in the face of his own death, Peter could even be funny. To the people of that day the cross was merely a sign of suffering and evil, the worst way to die. But to Peter and the Christians the cross had become something truly beautiful, for it opened the passage through death into the kingdom.

"I want one last favor," Peter asked the executioners. "Could you please crucify me upside down?" What a horrible request! Who would ask for more agony? "I've done things backward all my life," Peter explained. "It is only natural that I leave this world upside down. My Lord was crucified right side up. It wouldn't be fitting for me, who always went the wrong way, to die the same way."

The executioners granted Peter's wish. As he hung on the cross waiting for death, even at the end doing things the wrong way, Peter must have smiled through his great pain because he knew it was not so important to be right. The only really important thing was to love. He had learned that in the family of Jesus we all belong to: the church.

We Believe in the Forgiveness of Sins

If Peter could become a saint, we all should be able to do the same. We believe it is possible to change our lives and our ways of thinking. We believe in the forgiveness of sins.

Forgiving sins was an important part of Jesus' work. He told a story of a farmer who had two sons. The youngest son grew tired of the farm. He wanted to get out and see the world while he was still young, so he asked his father for his share of the family money. The father gave it to him and sadly watched as the young man packed and left for parts unknown.

All of that money soon burned a hole in the son's pocket. He spent it right and left. Soon it was gone and he had to work for a living. But there was a famine, food was scarce, and the son found himself working very hard for only pennies. He was feeding and taking care of pigs and eating the pigs' food just to survive.

One day he decided he'd had enough of this misery. Why, the people who work for my father live better than I do, he thought. There's no reason to stay here and kill myself. I'll go back home and ask my father for a job. It can't be any worse than this.

So the son started home. All the way he thought about what would happen when he arrived. He would have to talk fast to convince his father to hire him. He prepared his speech and rehearsed his lines over and over again so he got it right. "Father, I have sinned against you and against God. I no longer deserve to be called your son, but could you please take me on as one of your hired workers?" I don't know if it will do the trick, he thought, but there is nothing else I can do. It's all up to my father whether or not he accepts me back.

At last the old farmhouse came into sight. Now was the time. The son paused to take a deep breath and say a prayer. Then he began walking again. But what was this? Someone was running down the road toward him. Nobody knows I'm coming back, he thought. It looked like his father, but it couldn't be.

But it was his father. Every day his father had looked down that road hoping to see his son. Now, after all these years, his dreams were coming true: He ran up to the boy and embraced him. And the son, before anything could go wrong, tried to say his little speech, but his father stifled him with a bear hug. Before the boy could start again, his father was calling to the servants, "Kill the fatted calf! Let's have a celebration! My son has returned!"

A little later, the man's elder son finished his work and began to walk home from the fields. All those years he had done his duty. He had worked the farm and made it a success. Thank God I'm not like that shifty brat of a brother, he thought again and again. Where would Father be if it weren't for me? It's a good thing some people still have a sense of right and wrong. This elder brother felt pretty good about himself, and he should have: he had done a lot to help his father.

What is happening? he wondered. Why are all these decorations being put up? He questioned one of the servants.

"Why, your brother has come home, and your father has ordered a feast."

"Well, I'll just see about that," snorted the son, and he started off to find his father and settle things.

"What's the big deal?" he asked when he tracked down his father. "All these years I've slaved away for you and never once have you thrown a party for me and my friends. Yet this good-for-nothing son comes back home and you celebrate!"

"My son, look what has happened. For years we didn't know what had become of your brother. I feared he was dead, but I so wanted to see him again. And now look! He has come home. We thought he was dead, but he's alive. Come and join the celebration!"

He doesn't deserve to be forgiven, thought the elder brother. What will prevent him from worming himself back into the family and then doing the same thing again? I don't trust him. I wouldn't give an inch to him. He's had his chance and it's too bad. He's had his fun. Now let him learn his lesson. He needs a lot more hard work and suffering before I'd let him back.

But the elder brother was left alone. His father certainly didn't agree with him. Jesus doesn't think this way either. There are a lot of people who would agree with the elder brother, but Jesus calls this kind of thinking worldly thinking. He doesn't buy it.

Jesus prefers kingdom thought. He forgives that young man so that he can start over again. He forgives him totally even though there is no guarantee that the young man really learned his lesson. He forgives all of us so that we can learn to know the love our Father has for us and so that we can experience the joy of living as members of the kingdom rather than in the slavery of the world.

Jesus forgives us so that we can make a new start in life, so that we have a chance to leave behind our sinful ways of thinking and living and can begin to think and act in ways that bring happiness. We celebrate this wonderful forgiveness in the Sacrament of Baptism. When a person is baptized, all sins are forgiven. We can begin anew to seek the happiness our Father wants us to share.

even as much as seventy times seven

"Well," grumbled the elder brother, "I suppose just this once we can let the kid off the hook. But he better not do anything like it again, or he'll have to pay for it."

Some of the disciples thought as that elder brother. They loved the idea that Jesus went around forgiving sinners, as long as those sinners changed their lives. But what about those who didn't learn anything from all this forgiveness? What should be done if they went back to doing the things that had gotten them into trouble in the first place? Peter wondered about this, for Jesus had entrusted the task of forgiving sins to Peter and the other disciples.

"If you forgive people's sins, they are forgiven. If you hold them bound, they are held bound," Jesus had said.

That is a lot of power, thought Peter. I think I need a few guidelines on how we determine whether a person's sins should be forgiven.

Peter went to Jesus and asked, "Just how many times do I have to forgive someone before I can draw the line and say 'No more forgiveness for you'? Is seven times a good number? I would think that if they haven't learned to reform by the seventh time there is no hope they ever will."

"Not seven times, Peter. You must forgive seventy times seven," replied Jesus.

Jesus wants to give us every opportunity to be free of our sins. It is hard for us to forgive someone when they do something wrong to us. When we forgive them we are tempted to say, It's all right this time, but don't let it happen again. And if it does happen again, how easily can we forgive? It is difficult to forgive the second time, but Jesus tells us that our Father is willing to forgive not only the second time but every time. This forgiveness provides us with a perfect opportunity to turn from sin and enter into the happiness of the kingdom. In the church we experience that forgiveness in a special way through the Sacrament of Penance.

and healing as well

Jesus spent much of his time healing the blind, the lame, and the sick. We believe that his ministry continues in the church as we work for healing in our own lives, in those of our friends, and in society as well. As we have seen, our Father has always been concerned for the poor. He champions those who are powerless, those who have little to eat, those who are unable to provide for themselves and their families, and those who are in prison.

As Christians, we join ourselves with all the people in the world. If some do not have food or shelter, we try to help them. Just as Jesus went out of his way to be with the unfortunate, we as his disciples today work so that everyone will have enough to eat and will be protected from the suffering of disease and from the cruelty of being powerless to provide for themselves and their loved ones.

We believe that our Father heals his people. When we are ill, we don't give up hope. We pray that God will be with us in our illness. Sickness can be a time of growth and learning. If it had not been for their illnesses or handicaps, many of the people Jesus met would not have been able to enter the kingdom so easily. We see all the blind, the lame, and even the dead being healed by Jesus and seeing the kingdom. What of the people who were not ill, but who heard Jesus' words and saw his actions? Many of them believed, but to believe in Jesus is not the same as actually entering the kingdom. How many unafflicted people were as strongly changed as the blind person who saw because Jesus touched him?

Sickness for Christians is a time of learning. We call it a holy time because it can bring us close to God and open us to his healing power. Many Christians give their lives to the ministry of healing in medicine and nursing. All Christians in their prayer ask for healing for people and the world. When a Christian is seriously ill, the Christian community prays for healing and anoints the person with holy oil in the Sacrament of the Sick.

and we make our lives a thanksgiving to our Father

We move closer to the kingdom as we learn how to give thanks to our Father. During his life, Jesus was constantly giving thanks. He teaches us to give thanks daily in the Eucharist, for our attitude of unthankfulness can keep us blind to the love God is continuously showering upon us.

One day when Jesus was teaching on a hillside, many people followed to hear him speak. On this particular day, about five thousand people had gathered around Jesus. He had been teaching them all afternoon, and some of the disciples began to worry about how they would feed all these people. It was getting late and the village was quite a way off.

This was an important problem, so they approached Jesus to let him know the situation. Perhaps he would want to stop teaching now and send the crowd into town for food.

"Well, how much food did you bring for us?" Jesus asked.

"We've only got enough for ourselves: five loaves of bread and seven fish. There would never be enough for all these people," the disciples assured him.

"Bring me what you have," said Jesus. Obviously what they had was not enough. So often in our own lives we give up because we don't have enough to do what we want. We drop out of the race because we aren't good enough runners. We don't do well in school because we aren't smart enough. We don't help people because we don't have enough time or energy. We would like to do all these things, but, like the disciples, we can't because we don't have enough of what it takes.

Jesus doesn't agree with this kind of thinking. He would call it worldly thinking. It doesn't belong in the kingdom.

Jesus took those few loaves of bread, and he took the fish, and he didn't complain that there wasn't enough. He didn't agree with the disciples that the people would have to go searching for food.

Instead, Jesus took what he had and gave thanks

to his Father for what he had been given. What would happen if we began to do the same in our own lives? What if we gave thanks for our gift of running instead of complaining that we aren't good enough? What if we gave thanks for the intelligence we have instead of excusing ourselves because we aren't bright enough?

Jesus simply gave thanks for what he had been given. Then he did something even more daring and unusual. He took that small amount of bread and fish and broke it apart to pass among the crowd. The disciples wondered what in the world he hoped to accomplish. There wasn't enough food to whet an appetite let alone satisfy one. Didn't Jesus understand?

Yet when the food was passed around, everyone had enough to eat. There was more food left over than there was before the dinner began. What had happened? Could it be that Jesus' attitude of giving thanks can really make what we have enough? Could it be that if we gave thanks for what we have in our lives, miracles might begin to happen and we would see just how lavishly our Father provides for us? We can practice this act of giving thanks Jesus teaches us whenever we gather to celebrate the Eucharist.

so that others might come to see through us the light of the world

Our lives as Christians have a purpose. Jesus told the disciples that it was necessary for him to leave them so that the Holy Spirit could come upon them and guide them to the ends of the earth with their message of Good News. We too have learned the Good News of Jesus and his kingdom. We too believe that the kingdom offers us a happier life than we could have if we chose to live according to the rules of the world.

Jesus did not convince people of the joys of the kingdom by arguing with them. He showed them the glory of the kingdom in his own life. Jesus lived differently from the rest of us.

Once, the people wanted to condemn a woman they saw as a sinner. They brought Mary of Magdala to Jesus hoping he would give her over to the executioners. Instead, Jesus forgave her, and at that moment, she saw the kingdom and entered it.

The townspeople often thought that blind people were afflicted because they were being punished for their own sins or for the sins of their parents. But Jesus didn't explain things that way. He healed the blind, and they saw the kingdom and entered it.

The world believes that unless people are made to fear the law and the authorities, they will not obey and will do harm. Jesus did not believe this way. He loved people. He really loved them. And through him they saw how much better it was to live with love rather than with fear, and they entered into the Father's kingdom.

We believe in the kingdom Jesus showed us. In our own lives—through giving thanks, healing, forgiving, service to others, and love—we become windows through which other people can see the beauties of this kingdom and enter. We have a hard task. It is easier to speak about forgiving than it is to forgive. Yet we want to speak not with our tongues but with our lives. We dedicate ourselves to this mission. We give our lives to God to use as signs for his kingdom when we receive the Sacrament of Confirmation.

and we help bring the whole world into this kingdom through our service

Even more than giving thanks, giving service to others was the way Jesus lived. On the night before he died, he thought enough of his disciples to wash their feet before they all sat down to eat together. A teacher in Israel would never do this because it would be considered beneath him. Washing feet was something only a servant would do, yet here was Jesus, the teacher, putting on an apron and serving his friends.

The world teaches that the more powerful and noble we are the more we deserve to be waited on. If we have enough money, we can buy people to wait on us, and the world says we should do this. Our money says we deserve it. The world believes that if many people are dedicated to making our lives easier, we stand a better chance of being happy.

Jesus does not agree with this kind of thinking. In the kingdom, he says, the greatest person is the one who cares for and serves the most. It is not wrong for the teacher to be the servant of the disciples. It is the only way to live that will bring real happiness. As long as we put ourselves in the center of things, we will wonder why we are never satisfied, why we always feel something is missing. But when we put others in the center we find that miraculously we feel fulfilled. We can be happiest when we forget about our own comfort and spend our life helping others.

Our service to others helps us come to know and enter into the kingdom where we find our real happiness. Some Christians commit themselves to this ideal of service in a formal way through the Sacrament of Holy Orders. They learn to experience the kingdom by serving the other members of the church just as Jesus did when he washed his disciples' feet.

and above all by our love

We have seen how important it was to Jesus that Peter love him. It was even more important than Peter's doing the right thing. It was more important than Peter's denial that he had known Jesus. It was important enough to ask Peter three times, just to be sure.

We believe above all else that God our Father loves us. He loves us enough to speak to us through Jesus, and Jesus loves us enough to die on the cross so that we might be free of death. God loves us whether we know it or not, whether we like it or not. We can say that we don't want God to love us, but that doesn't change things. He still does. We can say that we do not love God, but that doesn't make any difference. He still loves us. When you love someone you can't decide not to love them. You're stuck. All you can do is love, no matter how the person you care for feels.

As Christians we know God loves us and we allow him to love us. We tell him we are willing to be loved. Through being loved by this wonderful Father, we, in turn, grow and learn to love.

Being loved can be dangerous because it changes us. When we allow ourselves to be loved, we are opening ourselves to change. For God's love is the Holy Spirit. When we allow God to love us, we invite the Holy Spirit into our hearts.

Soon the day arrives when not only are we loved but we begin to love in return. Now all sorts of new things start to happen, for we begin to believe that our beloved is the most wonderful person in all the universe. We want to be just like that person, so we begin to let go of ourselves and become more and more like the one we love.

The person we love, if they love us also, becomes more and more like us. God has already done that in Jesus. The love we share becomes an exciting adventure of growing and changing. Our life becomes happier and we begin to find ourselves more and more living in the kingdom.

Some Christians want to explore this adventure of love in a special way. As husband and wife they join together and promise they will love each other totally and freely forever. They make a home out of their love. And their love flows into their children, who come to see the beauty of love, and out into their friends and neighbors, who come to see the kingdom in this couple. Such an adventure is the Sacrament of Christian Marriage.

We Believe in the Resurrection of the Body

Just as Jesus passed through death and entered completely into his Father's kingdom, we believe that at the end of our earthly life he will bring us into the full happiness he has promised us. In our Father's kingdom we will know the joy we only experience partly here on earth. And since our bodies are so wonderful, we believe that in the kingdom they will be transformed and made glorious, so that we will live in a much more marvelous way than we do now.

Jesus' mother Mary was completely open to God. She lived her life to do God's will. And at the end of her life she was assumed, body and soul, into the kingdom. The rest of creation must await the full and final coming of the kingdom at the end of the world before our bodies are resurrected and glorified. In Mary's Assumption we can see what has been promised to us on that day, after the Last Judgment, when the world passes away and the kingdom of our Father replaces it.

We can prepare ourselves for this marvelous Resurrection by opening our lives to God. Like Mary, we can seek to follow and to do the will of our Father rather than ourselves. If we believe Jesus can really make us happy, we have all the more reason to live the way he showed us rather than the way we would choose ourselves. When we open ourselves to

God, we move that much closer to the kingdom and the real happiness God wishes to be ours.

And Life Everlasting

Mary showed us how our own lives and the world will eventually turn out. For she, and we, are the reason God created the kingdom in the first place. He created the kingdom out of his love for us.

As we have seen, we can tell the history of our life with God as an ancient and popular story. In the beginning, God created us out of his love. He was deeply in love with us, and he hoped we might love him in return, but we were not ready to fall in love just yet. We wanted to find out things for ourselves, so the human race fell into sin. We adopted all the ways of thinking and acting that led to our unhappiness and led us to hurt one another and make ourselves miserable.

But God still ached for us to return his love and join together with him. He told Israel of his love and showed her the way to live so that she might be happy. That way of life is contained in the Law and the Ten Commandments, but such a life was too difficult for Israel and she failed again and again. Of all the people in Israel, only Mary was so trusting that she gave herself completely to God. She consented to be the mother of Jesus. And through Jesus, God came among us as a human being in no way different from us except that he did not think and act sinfully.

In his miracles and his teaching Jesus showed us a different way of living. Our Father was inviting us to share in this happy way of life that Jesus called the kingdom. Finally Jesus gave his own life so that we could give up our fear and enter the kingdom. He destroyed death through his cross and Resurrection. He showed us we need not be afraid of death. We can trust him to lead us through death and into the life of the kingdom.

At the end of her life, God called Mary home to the kingdom to live and reign with him over all creation. The story is not completed because all of us have not yet left the world behind for the kingdom. The day when all of God's beloved creation comes back to him and enters the kingdom is still far off, but we can see now what will happen on that wonderful day. When Mary was taken to the kingdom she was crowned the Queen of Heaven. And when all the rest of her sisters and brothers come into the kingdom, we will share her reign.

Our story will have a happy ending. God's love will be able to win us all over, and like Mary, we will fall in love with God. We all know that when we fall in love wonderful things happen. Body and soul we will enter into the kingdom and, with God, rule over all creation. If this were a story of the world, we could say now that they lived happily ever after, but it is a story of the kingdom so we say that we will live life everlasting.

# 5.

Bringing the Creed into Our Hearts

We have explored the different phrases of the Creed. Now we know what they mean. If we believe the truths in this short Creed, they will bring us happiness. The Creed teaches us what the world is like, who we are, and where we are going.

How can we make all the things we have learned in the Creed a real part of our thinking and living? How can we learn the Creed not only in our heads but in our hearts as well? In the story of Jesus' birth, after the shepherds have left to go back to the fields, we read that "Mary pondered all these things in her heart." She reflected and remembered again and again what had happened to her, and her pondering revealed more and more of God's love. We can imitate Mary's way of praying when we pray a special prayer dedicated to her called the Rosary. Through this prayer we can enter into the story of Jesus' life again and again throughout our own lives. We will ponder the events of Jesus' life in our hearts, and we will come to know God and his love for us ever more wonderfully.

The Rosary is a chain of beads that we use to guide us in our meditation. We begin at the cross on the chain. As we hold the cross, we make the cross and pray the Creed that we have studied in this book. We begin our prayer by reviewing those truths by which we live and in which we hope.

Now we move from the cross to the first large bead. On each of the large beads we will pray the special prayer Jesus taught us: the Lord's Prayer.

Our Father
who art in heaven
hallowed be thy name.
Thy kingdom come,
thy will be done
   on earth as it is in heaven.
Give us this day our daily bread,
and forgive us our trespasses
   as we forgive those who trespass
     against us.
And lead us not into temptation
   but deliver us from evil.

Let us take our time each time we pray the Lord's Prayer in the Rosary. Let us pray slowly, as if we were praying it for the first time and think about what the words mean. We let the words call forth our own feelings and hopes. We let the words become our own words. We feel what we are praying. We allow our hearts to open to our Father. We let the words of Jesus be a guide for what we want to tell him.

Now we move to the first group of three small beads. We honor Mary by saying the Hail Mary at each of the small beads of the Rosary.

> Hail Mary,
> full of grace.
> The Lord is with you.
> Blessed are you among women,
> and blessed is the fruit of your
> womb, Jesus.
> Holy Mary,
> Mother of God,
> pray for us sinners now
> and at the hour of our death.

We pray this differently from the Lord's Prayer. The Hail Mary is a prayer that can help us create a soothing and steady rhythm so that, like Mary, we can ponder the stories of Jesus. We pray the Hail Mary quickly, not thinking of each word. We say the prayer over and over again, and the rhythm of the words creates a stillness and peace in which we can enter our hearts and ponder the stories.

In the first group of three Hail Marys, we ask Mary to help us pray as she did. We ask her to guide us in our meditations. We ask her to bring us close to her and to Jesus so that we might learn to love and trust God as she did. Mary said yes with all her life when God asked her to be the mother of Jesus. She gave Jesus to the world. As Christians we hope to give Jesus to the world too. We can only do this if, like Mary, we learn how to say yes to God's love. As we pray the Rosary we open our hearts to God and become more willing to do his will rather than our own.

After the third bead, there is a little space of chain. We have now completed our opening prayers, and so we honor the Trinity by praying the hymn of praise, the Doxology.

> Glory be to the Father, and to the Son,
> and to the Holy Spirit,
> As it was in the beginning,
> is now and ever shall be,
> world without end. Amen.

We will end each of our meditations with this prayer, for Jesus has shown us that the true way to live and be happy is to give thanks and praise to God.

When we come to the medal on the Rosary that begins the circle of beads, we begin our meditations on the life of Jesus and Mary. First we must decide which five scenes we will choose for our meditation. All together there are fifteen different meditations in the Rosary. They are joined in three groups which we call the Joyful Mysteries, the Sorrowful Mysteries, and the Glorious Mysteries. Each of the mysteries is one of the stories we have heard as we studied our Creed. Each mystery brings us into a special moment in the life of Jesus or Mary.

The Joyful Mysteries are about the birth of Jesus. The first is the Annunciation, when the angel appeared to Mary and told her she would give birth to Jesus (page 59). The Visitation shows Mary visiting her cousin Elizabeth with her Good News (page 60). The third mystery is the birth of Jesus in the stable (page 63). Next we see Mary and Joseph taking Jesus to the temple where Simeon sees him and speaks of him (page 64). Finally, we enter the story of Jesus going to the temple when he is twelve and teaching the doctors of the Law (page 11).

The Sorrowful Mysteries are about the Passion and death of Jesus. First we join with him in his agony in the garden (page 68). We see him whipped and beaten (page 69). Then Jesus is crowned with thorns (page 70). In the fourth mystery, he is forced to carry his own cross (page 71). And finally, he is crucified (page 72).

The Glorious Mysteries are about the Resurrection and the wonderful ending in store for us in our Father's kingdom. The first mystery is the Resurrection of Jesus (page 76). Then Jesus ascends into heaven (page 78). The third mystery is the Holy Spirit's descent upon the disciples at Pentecost (page 86); and the last two mysteries are about Mary's Assumption into heaven (page 110) and Mary's being crowned the Queen of Heaven (page 112).

Now we decide which of these three sets of mysteries we want to meditate on today. Many people pray the Joyful Mysteries on Monday and Wednesday, the Sorrowful Mysteries on Tuesday and Friday, and the Glorious Mysteries on Wednesday, Saturday, and Sunday. Around Christmas, we pray the Joyful Mysteries; during Lent we concentrate on the Sorrowful Mysteries; and during Easter time and at other times of the year we can focus on the Glorious Mysteries.

Once we have chosen which set of mysteries we want to pray, we move to the first large bead on the circle. Once again we pray the Lord's Prayer. We pray it slowly, listening to the words, responding to the words. We make these words of Jesus our own, and we let them call us into prayer.

Now we announce the first mystery. For example: The angel tells Mary she will give birth to Jesus the savior. We pause for just a moment, let that scene appear to us, and move to the first of the ten small beads. On each of these beads, we pray the Hail Mary, not listening to the words now. We pray quickly. With some practice we can develop a certain rhythm of saying this prayer and we let that rhythm soothe us. When the prayer is finished, we move to the next bead and repeat it.

The Hail Marys create a musical background to our meditation. While our lips and fingers move through the ten Hail Marys, we enter into the mystery we are pondering.

Allow the scene to appear to you. Who is present? Imagine all the details you can. For example: What is Mary wearing? What does she look like? Where is she? What time of day is it? How does the angel appear? What does he say to Mary? How does she respond to the angel?

During your meditation, enter into the story and play with it. Have fun imagining all the details. Become one of the characters in the story and relive the story from that person's point of view. In the Annunciation, you might take the part of Mary or of the angel. You will find that with just a little practice you can create a real picture in your mind. Then you can enjoy it, explore it, and be refreshed by it whenever you want.

Whenever we pray the Rosary, each time we return to a mystery, we can create and enter the mystery in a different way. The possibilities are only limited by our own imaginations.

At the end of the ten small beads there is another stretch of chain. It is now time to end this meditation. We pause a moment to leave the scene, and end the meditation by praying the Doxology. We praise and thank God for what we have learned and experienced in this mystery.

Now once again we find a large bead. Once more we pray the Lord's Prayer as we did before the first mystery. We announce the second mystery, and we proceed in this way through all five mysteries until we reach the medal again. If it is bedtime, to conclude our Rosary at the medal, we might say the prayer of Simeon.

> Now, all powerful Master,
> you allow your servant to depart in peace;
> for you have been faithful to your promise.
> My eyes have seen your saving action
> which you have shown to all the peoples:
> A light to guide the nations
> and give glory to Israel, your people.

Or we could pray Mary's prayer as she gives thanks to God for all he has done for her. This prayer is called the Magnificat:

My heart gives praise to the Lord,
> my soul rejoices in God my savior.

He notices me in my humility;
> from now on everyone will call me
> > the happiest person.

The one who can do anything has
> done great things for me.

May his name be holy!

All through the ages he shows mercy
> to those who fear him.

He puts forth his mighty arm
> and scatters the mighty and
> > powerful.

He throws kings from their thrones
> and lifts up the poor and humble.

He feeds the hungry with good things
> and sends the rich away with empty
> > hands.

He has helped Israel, his child,
> and he has remembered his mercy

the mercy he promised to our fathers
> and mothers,
> > to Abraham and his children
> > > forever.

All through our lives the Rosary can journey with us as our friend in prayer. It will help us make the truths of the Creed into the heart of our life. When we are troubled and discouraged, the Sorrowful Mysteries will give us courage and hope. In times of joy, the mysteries of Jesus' birth can help us celebrate. And the Glorious Mysteries can be our constant reminder of the wonderful things God has prepared to share with us in his kingdom.

The Rosary depends on what we bring to it. It is not a mere repetition of prayers but rather a joyful way to come closer to the truths Jesus shows to us. As we enter the scenes of the Rosary, we too can meet Jesus, and we can be taught, forgiven, and healed by him. We too can feel, taste, and see the kingdom. Through the Rosary, we can receive the real and lasting happiness our Father wishes to be ours.